Praise
for
Stories We Didn't Tell

"Anna Citrino's *Stories We Didn't Tell* lifts history up from the land and out of the history books to render it intimate and marvelously lyrical. Meticulously researched and packed with incidents and insights from the poet's in-depth interviews, this book of poems is as immersive as a great novel and yet is first and foremost a poetic investigation presented in taut lines, breathtaking images that shimmer with both meaning and consequence, and a profluence that won't let you stop reading. A remarkable reading experience. A brilliant literary accomplishment."

RENEE ASHLEY, author of *Minglements:
Prose on Poetry and Life*

"In *Stories We Didn't Tell*, Anna Citrino tells a story of her own family, and in so doing, tells the story of women's struggle for equality, the story of America, and how things changed over the course of the 20th century. It's written as a book, and one I'm sure you'll keep reading straight through as I did. It's a story of determination and pluck and sorrow. I loved reading this book; I was drawn into the characters, the lives they lived, the difficulties they experienced, as well as the beauty they found in the ugliest moments of their lives. What a wonderful book!"

MARIA MAZZIOTTI GILLAN,
winner of the American Book Award

"In *Stories We Didn't Tell*, poet Anna Citrino uses her own carefully researched family history to bring to life in verse the indomitable pioneering spirit of a Nebraska and Wyoming family. Poetry liberates the storytelling because this collection of inhabited narrators share their stories on the page with an emotional heft that only a deft poet crafting lines in couplets, tercets, and quatrains can convey. These narrators move us along the twentieth century facing two world wars, the meaning of work, harsh natural elements and judgments, and the finding and exercising female agency. Citrino gives us a universal story, even if our own families did not participate in homesteading and the westward movement. This collection provides an album of voices we can hear and cherish."

BARBARA KRASNER, author of *Ethel's Song: Ethel Rosenberg's Life in Poems*, co-winner of The Paterson Prize for Books for Young People, Grades 7–12

"'The past is never dead, it's not even past,' wrote William Faulkner. In brilliant, profound, and lyrical poems, Citrino imagines and tells unspoken stories that plumb the soul and psyche of American settlers. A masterful book with sweeping scope and depth, *Stories We Don't Tell* expresses the courage, daring, and despair of Americans settling the West. The themes in this book are as relevant today as ever. I can't imagine a more wide-ranging history of western expansion with its undercurrents and repercussions. A novel-like book of poems—in a genre all its own—*Stories We Don't Tell* weaves together personal tales about people whose lives reflect the changing political and social landscape of the United States. At the book's core is the question, 'When and how do we become ourselves?' Citrino explores all this in her beautiful, crisp, and spare style—stunning and often breathtaking, an important and powerful book that offers hope to the human spirit."

SUSAN G. WOOLDRIDGE, author of *poemcrazy: freeing your life with words*

"Anna Citrino's astonishing new book, *Stories We Didn't Tell*, is the story of a family of poor homesteaders on the Great Plains that spans both world wars. The story is told through poems, arranged into chapters, that carry the reader along with as much narrative suspense and immersion as any traditional novel. The poems, spoken by family members, shimmer with the authenticity of living voices, allowing intimate access to the inner lives of the speakers as they try to make meaning of their lives amidst the many hardships they face, including unforgiving weather and equally unforgiving economic and social strictures, especially for women. So alive are these voices, it's as if a time machine had dropped me into the pages of this book where I was able to see through the eyes of the characters and almost feel the blood coursing through their veins as they react to their own behaviors and thoughts and to the events unfolding in their daily lives. One of the characters says, 'Most of us don't know much about the truth of our own stories, much less questions of destiny.' Through Adah, the central character, I bore witness to one woman's struggle to step outside her seemingly pre-ordained life of deprivation and subservience. Despite the brutality of two events that occurred in her youth, she finds the strength to forge a life of some independence and even beauty, something she longed for since we first meet her at eight years old, marveling at the 'Sun-warmed fields dotted with coneflowers. I left *Stories We Didn't Tell* knowing a great deal more about my own story and believing that destiny is based in human rights, not in the supernatural."

LINDA HILLRINGHOUSE, author of
The Things I Didn't Know to Wish For

"The cyclical nature of drought, crop failures, illness, starvation, and the hard labor of farming that never ends, counterbalanced by tenacity, love of family, and the solace of nature are pieced together like a quilt to tell the story that begins with a family settling on the Great Plains at the turn of the 20th century and ends in 1983. Spurred by the desire to start fresh by farming on an unforgiving land, *Stories We Didn't Tell* lifts the veil and reveals the personal story of one family—a story that could have been lost forever if not for the poetry of Anna Citrino. She follows her family as they leave the plains, scatter across state lines, and try to build their own diverse lives. She gives voice to every member of her family that settled in Nebraska and Wyoming. Her use of dramatic monologues allows the reader to dive deeply into the psyche and lived experiences of her family members. The poems are filled with grace and skill in such a way that we are living each family member's life and gaining an intimate understanding of their unforgettable hardships and joys. We all have stories our families will not tell, and we should follow in Citrino's footsteps and excavate our stories. From reading these poems, I feel connected to her family and therefore, connected to the world. Citrino writes, 'Stories help us understand ourselves and our place in the world. They connect us with others across time and place. In the world my parents grew up in, people didn't talk about their inner lives, struggles, or histories. Hardships were simply part of life and required quiet acceptance.' Our family stories are part of our history, and the struggles of our ancestors are imprinted on each of us. *Stories We Didn't Tell* gifts us with an epic of an ordinary family and shares with us their extraordinary lives."

KATHLEEN WILLARD, author of *The Next Noise Is Our Hearts* and *This Incendiary Season*

"This vivid novel-in-verse offers up a character for the ages. Adah faces more than her fair share of sorrows, but perseveres. Through personal and historical traumas, Adah is resilience personified. This is her story, but it is also more broadly a portrait of women making their way in a world set against them. Anna Citrino has created something truly special in *Stories We Don't Tell*. This epic tale of family and survival in the Great Plains is exceptional."

ERICA WRIGHT, author of *All the Bayou Stories End with Drowned*

"*Stories We Didn't Tell* is a compelling portrait of the individual, the family, and the human spirit. Citrino's exquisitely crafted poems follow members of one family over nearly a century as they navigate experiences from the mundane to the tragic to the transcendent. For Citrino's characters, actions such as washing or cooking become metaphors, ways for them to express the things they do not—or cannot—say to one another. To the readers, of course, her characters lay bare their inmost thoughts, grappling with questions of freedom, power, gender roles, nature, parenting, aging. The result is a work that is simultaneously gentle and piercing, a profoundly moving look at the extraordinary depths of ordinary people."

GINNY KUBITZ MOYER,
author of *A Golden Life*

Stories
we didn't tell

Anna Citrino

SHANTI ARTS PUBLISHING
BRUNSWICK, MAINE

Stories We Didn't Tell

Copyright © 2025 Anna Citrino

All Rights Reserved
No part of this document may be reproduced or transmitted in any form or by any means without prior written permission of the publisher, except in the case of brief quotations embodied in critical reviews.

Published by Shanti Arts Publishing
Designed by Shanti Arts Designs

Nicholas Samaras, "Ars Poetica as Reconstruction"
Used with permission of the poet

Cover image by Anna Citrino and used with her permission

Shanti Arts LLC
193 Hillside Road
Brunswick, Maine 04011
shantiarts.com

Printed in the United States of America

ISBN: 978-1-962082-75-4 (softcover)

Library of Congress Control Number: 2025942595

*For my great aunt Anna,
my mother, Frances,
and my aunt Ruth*

CONTENTS

ACKNOWLEDGMENTS	15
PREFACE	19
FAMILY TREE	21

ONE—PRAIRIE, 1897–1901

NEBRASKA PRAIRIE	26
ABOUT CHILDHOOD	27
ADAH BREAKS A RULE	29
THINGS WE DON'T TALK ABOUT—	
WHAT JASPER TOLD ADAH	32
SURVIVAL METHODS	33
ADELLA'S ADVICE	36

TWO—STORM, 1903–1908

WIND RISE	42
WHAT DID I KNOW?	44
JED PONDERS MANIFEST DESTINY	47
LENORE'S WISH	49
HOW WINTER ARRIVED	51
ADAH MAKES A QUILT WITH LENORE	53
JED GOES FOR A WALK	55
AS WE ARE	58
DAYDREAMING WITH CLOUDS	60

THREE—DROUGHT, 1908

DURING DROUGHT	64
CONSIDERING WHAT HAPPENED	66
COMING TO TERMS	67
ADELLA ASSISTS ADAH GIVING BIRTH	69
KNOTS	70
THE BLUE DRESS	71

FOUR—EDGES, 1908–1915

BEGINNING NEW	76
WHEN ADAH MET GERARD	77
GERARD'S ABSENCE	79
OBSERVATIONS	80
THE EDGE OF A NEW BEGINNING	81
CARVING	83
BARN DANCE WITH THE FAMILY	86

SPEAKING OF DESIRE	88
DECISION	90
OUR STARTING DESTINATION	93

FIVE—CLOUDS, 1916–1918

WHY EDRA MARRIED AUGUST	98
GERARD'S NEW BUSINESS	100
CONFESSION	101
A FINAL RECOGNITION	103
PREPARING FOR CLASS	105
ADELLA WATCHES CLOUDS WITH JASPER	107
THE SHIFT	108
GARDENING	110

SIX—LOVE AND WORK, 1919–1929

LAUNDRY WOMEN, ADAH'S WORK	114
JAMIE'S QUESTION	116
WHAT SEPTEMBER'S LIGHT SUGGESTED	118
MY MOTHER'S HANDS	120
ADAH AND JAMIE'S NEW ROLE	122
A PROPER WOMAN	124
A WOMAN WITH SASS	127
THE PANTS I WEAR	129
THE GEOMETRY OF LOVE	131
CELEBRATING THE ORDINARY	133

SEVEN—TURNINGS, 1930–1935

PLANING WOOD	138
FIGHT	139
THOUGHTS WHILE WALKING	141
WHAT HAPPENED TO FRANK	144
THE CHRISTMAS MOTHER	148
AVERY'S INSIGHT	150
LEITH'S NEW OPPORTUNITY	151
REMEMBERING ADELLA	154
MATTERS OF CHOICE, ADAH'S NEW WORLD	156

EIGHT—DUST, 1936–1944

THE HEART OF SOMEWHERE	160
MISTAKE	162
DUST	164
AFTER DANCING	166

JAMIE CONSIDERS ADAH'S DECISION	169
PERSPECTIVE	171
WHY AUGUST LEFT EDRA	175
EDRA'S RIDE	177
WISHING	179

NINE—WIND, 1945–1952

BUILDING BRIDGES	184
WHY DID I MARRY YOU? DRAFT FOR AN ANNIVERSARY LETTER	186
THE TREES	188
IN THE PLAINS OF WIND	190
NOT JUST ANOTHER MORNING	192
ROCK HUNTING	194
DEFINITIONS	196
SOMETHING ABOUT ASH	198

TEN—MENDING, 1953–1965

A SLOW FULLNESS	204
WHAT JAMIE WAITED TO HEAR	205
LISTENING LONG AND FAR	207
SWEET DAYS	210
EDRA SITS FOR A PHOTO	212
AFTER LITTON, ADAH REFLECTS ON HER THIRD MARRIAGE	214
A RETURN TO REFUGE, ADAH'S PLAN	219

ELEVEN—QUILT, 1966–1983

THERE'S NOT ENOUGH SUGAR IN THIS WORLD	220
PATCHWORK	222
MARGOT'S DISCOVERY	224
HANGING LAUNDRY	226
CEDRIC MEETS WITH ADAH AND JAMIE	228
A CAT COMES TO ADAH	230
QUILT	233
MOON LANDING, MINI SKIRTS, AND OTHER TRANSFORMATIONS	235
STANDING IN THE MIDDLE OF A GREAT FIELD	238
TIMELINE	241
AFTERWORD	249
ABOUT THE AUTHOR	253

ACKNOWLEDGMENTS

Grateful recognition is given to the editors of these literary periodicals in which the following poems originally appeared, though at times with a slightly different form or title:

Bellowing Ark: "Adah's Nebraska Prairie", "Adella's Advice"; "The Christmas Mother"; and "Rock Hunting"
Evening Street Review: "Adah Talks About Childhood"
Indelible: "Edra Describes Why She Married August"
Pasque Petals: "Adella Watches Clouds With Jasper" and "The Geometry of Love"
Paterson Literary Review: "Gardening"
Poppy Road Review: "Avery's Insight" and "A Slow Fullness"
Porter Gulch Review: "Edra Sits for a Photo" and "Jamie's Question"
Waterwheel Review: "Remembering Adella"
The Main Street Rag: "The Shift"
They Call Us: "Adah and Jamie's New Role"
Writing in a Woman's Voice: "After Litton"; "Mistake"; "Observations"; "Quilt"; "Speaking of Desire"; and "What Jamie Waited to Hear"

While cooking his breakfast on Saturday mornings, I recall my father reciting poems he had memorized as a young man working on a sheep wagon in South Dakota. He also loved writing poetry that I treasured reading. Alive to the natural world, my mother listened carefully and observed it closely. I'm forever grateful for the gifts of my parents' presence and way of being. Together they nurtured the writer in me.

I'm deeply grateful to Aunt Ruth, Uncle Clifford, and Aunt Kay for so generously sharing their stories of family memories and history with me. Also, thank you to my cousin Georgia for recollections she shared about grandparents and relatives.

My enormous gratitude to Michael Citrino for his patient and spacious heart, perceptive suggestions, and deep, listening ear as I read each poem aloud to him in their draft forms, often numerous times. My sincere appreciation to Michael L. Newell who read every poem in this manuscript as I first wrote them. His ongoing responses to my writing over two and a half decades and his affirmation of my writing efforts have been an immeasurable support.

Deep gratitude to my publisher, Christine Brooks Cote, editor and publisher of Shanti Arts Publishing and *Still Point Arts Quarterly* for the great gift of her belief in this book's story. Her time, effort, and support have allowed this book to become a physical reality.

Thank you to Erica Wright for her helpful observations and comments on the manuscript's first draft. A bow to Renee Ashley for her generous and valuable suggestions on an early draft of the manuscript. I'm deeply thankful for her heartfelt, encouraging remarks that helped me to persevere as I revised. I also wish to thank Linda Hillringhouse for her discerning ear, abundantly helpful suggestions, and ongoing responses to many of these poems. Her generous support of my writing effort has been invaluable. My sincere appreciation goes out to Carole Oles who graciously volunteered to read a draft of this manuscript and offered valuable comments that helped me focus on specific areas for revision. Thank you to Susan G. Wooldridge for her encouragement, support, and steadfast belief in the value of this manuscript.

My heartfelt appreciation to Carol Keeney, Mary Catherine Frazier, and Richard Frazier for their generous interest and support, and for Catherine's specific and helpful suggestions that encouraged me to further develop Adah's story. My sincere appreciation to Lisa O'Hara for her observations and comments on the first section of poems, and to Pegatha Hughes for her suggestions on an earlier draft of the manuscript. I'm grateful to Theresa Roach Melia for her encouragement as she listened to me read these poems. I send my appreciation as well to Shelly Shephard, Mona Gibson James, and Janice Debo for cheering me on as they read and responded to a variety of these poems. I extend my appreciation to members of Redwood Writers Salon and Circle gatherings for their supportive comments to several of the poems that appear in this book. Thank you to Beate Sigriddaughter for publishing several poems in this volume in her electronic journal, *Writing in a Woman's Voice*, and for generously encouraging me with the November 2023 Moon Prize for the poem "Speaking of Desire." Thank you to Jerry Austin and the folks at Bellowing Ark for their ongoing support of my writing. My appreciation goes out to Maria Gomez for her research suggestion, and my heartfelt gratitude to Sharman Murphy, a poet friend who always encouraged my writing efforts.

My sincere gratitude to family members, specifically Lynda and Steve McCluer, and dear friends Jennifer and Greg Hellman, who graciously listened to a draft of this book as I read it aloud. The gift of their listening ears and heartfelt support was of great value in helping me see how I wanted to develop and revise the manuscript.

To all of my teachers, workshop leaders, and friends who have helped me grow as a writer, in particular: Jeannine Bohlmeyer, my first poetry teacher; Nicholas Samaras, an expert teacher whose generous feedback on my work has made me a better writer; and Maria Mazziotti Gillan, for her continuous encouragement; as well as every one of my readers for their support of my work—thank you.

PREFACE

Dear Reader,

Stories help us to understand ourselves and our place in the world. They connect us with others across time and place. In the world my parents grew up in, people didn't talk about their inner lives, struggles, or histories. Hardships were simply part of life and required quiet acceptance. In *Stories We Didn't Tell*, I recover voices once denied space, story, and life to give them light and breath.

Shortly before I was born, my parents moved from where they were raised in South Dakota to California. As the first child born outside of my parents' native area, I grew up living in two worlds, so to speak. At home I was living in South Dakota, subject to my parents' thinking and values of hard work and quiet acceptance of life's daily tasks. Outside the home, I was living in southern California with its diverse way of being in the world.

Wanting to understand the place and people I came from, I set out on a journey to know my heritage. This book is a result of that journey. In the summer of 1995, I visited Wyoming and South Dakota. My mother's sister chauffeured me around the countryside so that I could stand in the locations where my grandparents and great-grandparents lived and worked. I wanted to absorb the landscape, let its presence sink into my bones. The conversations and interviews during that stay with my aunt, a few of my uncles, and my aunt's friend—a local historian living in Cheyenne, Wyoming—gave me a sense of my ancestors' lives and stories.

Stories We Didn't Tell is quilted together from interviews with relatives, letters and documents from family members, extensive research gathered from books and online articles, scholarly resources, as well as various websites and videos connected to the era. These helped me to construct the social and environmental context of events and experiences portrayed in these poems. The core of events presented here is real; however, I changed characters' names to protect descendants' privacy and invented scenes around basic information I gathered. What you read is a work of imagination breathing into factual information.

When examined closely, the story of people and places that might seem ordinary can often be quite extraordinary if one looks at events in their larger context and probes beneath their surfaces. *Stories We Didn't Tell* carries readers into the world of common people who struggle to make a meaningful life despite confining social roles, gender expectations, and economic challenges. Perseverance inside a changing land, the unraveling of traditional ways, and movement toward modernity—this is the world *Stories We Didn't Tell* explores.

While today the western states of Nebraska, Wyoming, and South Dakota are sometimes looked upon as America's bland backcountry, the unfolding of the American West in these states was foundational to today's modern America and is central to understanding who we are as Americans. As Nicholas Samaras writes in his poem, "Ars Poetica as Reconstruction,"

> I write to recognize and hold on. I write for wholeness.
>
> I write to live through time
> and breathe life into that time again.

Though you may not be the descendant of settlers, I hope you'll find something of your own stories and the story of America inside the poems in this book and discover a possibility of greater wholeness.

Thank you for reading,

Anna Citrino

FAMILY TREE

Jasper (father) ——— m. 1887 ——— **Adella** (mother)
b. 1847 — d. 1918   b. 1857 — d. 1935
                                               m. **Joel** 1922

    Rhoda (daughter)   b. 1879 — d. 1885

    Shara (daughter)   b. 1881 — d. 1900

    Lenore (daughter)   b. 1883 — d. 1948
        m. **Jed** 1906
        adopted **Margot** 1908

    Leith (son)   b. 1886 — d. 1967
        m. **Brielle** 1915
        adopted **Kent** 1924

    Adah (daughter)   b. 1889 — d. 1986
        m. **Claude** 1905
        m. **Gerard** 1909
        m. **Raymond** 1936
        divorced **Raymond** 1936
        m. **Litton** 1937

    Avery (son)   b. 1893 — d. 1972

    Edra (daughter)   b. 1895 — d. 1971
        m. **August** 1916
        daughter **Frieda** b. 1919
        daughter **Riva** b. 1924

    Jamie (daughter)   b. 1897 — d. 1987
        m. **Howard** 1925
        divorced **Howard** 1926
        m. **Frank** 1926
        m. **Alfred** 1928

    Cedric (son)   b. 1899 — d. 1981
        m. **Della** 1927

The past is never behind us, it's actually within us.
—Michael Meade

... for the growing good of the world is partly dependent on unhistoric acts; and that things are not so ill with you and me as they might have been, is half owing to the number who lived faithfully a hidden life, and rest in unvisited tombs.
—George Eliot, *Middlemarch*

There is no greater agony than bearing an untold story inside you.
—Maya Angelou

One

Prairie
1897–1901

NEBRASKA PRAIRIE

Crawford, Nebraska, 1897
Adah, age 8

Mother always had her head bent to her work,
Father to the fields.
The whole family had chores.
Mine were to help Mama sweep, cook,
hang laundry, iron, do needlework, carry water,
wood—do anything my parents asked.
Work was our way, and we pressed
into its weight.

But I loved to escape to the fields.
When I could, I'd dash out the door
   swallowing big draughts of air,
      run and run till my legs hurt
         and muscles ached,
the family's kinks and knots loosening
until, too tired to run further,
   I'd lie down in the wheatfields
to rest, let the earth   seep into me
and listen to the wheat stalks
scratch against each other in the wind.

Sun-warmed fields dotted with coneflowers,
and black-eyed Susans, bee dance,
   the swirl of painted lady butterflies,
leaping grasshoppers, or a red-winged
blackbird's flutter—this is the world that held
and lifted me
     into a warbler's high-pitched song,
        or a bluebird's *tru-lee.*

Speckled with pink prairie phlox or purple mallow,
whatever the day's harsh words or repetitive chores,
the fields in their freshness waited, ready to hold me
in their wide laps and ease.

ABOUT CHILDHOOD

Crawford, Nebraska, January 1901
Adah, age 12

It was winter, 1901.
I wore a path through the snow where I carried
water for washing, pouring it into my employer's
washtub, then scrubbed the clothes across the board.

The previous day's laundry dry from the room's
warm fire waited in a nearby basket. Coals burned
red in the iron, and I began pressing the wrinkles
from the men's shirts the way Mama taught me.

It was hard work lifting the iron's heavy weight,
keeping the coals inside at a constant temperature,
while moving it steadily along to not scorch the fabric.

Mama never taught me about men,
how they could burn a crease into me
that didn't release with washing.

My brother, my father, they weren't like
those at the house where my parents sent me to work.

Father had his rules for keeping things straight.
"Difficult land requires discipline," he'd say,
and had us practice determination every day
to keep our will strong.

I willed myself to lift that iron
long after my arm was tired, smoothing over
wrinkled cloth after washing every soiled surface,
even after that man entered the room where I worked,
me thinking he wanted only to add some further
direction, or give me an additional piece to wash.

(continued)

"Stand still," he told me as I struggled.
His acrid sweat. The way he pushed me away
afterwards saying, "Wash up now. Gotta keep
everything clean."

I tried, but couldn't tell my tears from the water,
couldn't remove the room's dank smell
or rid his grit from my neck.

Many times, I've heated an iron, wrestled
its weight up and down that event's fabric,
but never could extract its stain or make
that memory's wrinkled crease turn smooth.

I tried. But I never did feel clean.
Only thing that disappeared
was my childhood.

ADAH BREAKS A RULE

Crawford, Nebraska, January 1901
Adah, age 12

Nebraska's near decade of drought brought
failed crops, failed businesses and banks.
Droves fell into homelessness.

Farmers shot their hogs to keep them from starving.
We worked, ate as we could, and did as we were told,
believing obedience to our continued effort
could save us.

"Please" and "thank you" were not spoken at our meals.
Sitting wasn't allowed. Our plates were full
of silence, our house functioned on Father's rules.

The morning's fine snow had turned fierce.
Wind rolled over the world, groaned,
thrust brute hands against the house, a freeze
so cold it adhered to the house's rough-sawn boards
and collected in my bones.

Shuddering, I stared at my plate poking the potatoes
before lifting them to my mouth to choke them down
past the rocks stuck in my throat.

A fork clanked. Images from that afternoon
surfaced instantly—the jangled cry of the man's belt
as it clashed on the laundry tub. The iron's heat
I'd set nearby to use on newly laundered clothes
too near my face, ready to burn. His shirt's
jittery movement rubbing my neck
as he squeezed into me.

I couldn't swallow.
Formless howls pushed against my chest
clawed their way up my throat
wanting to cry out. *(continued)*

Someone nearby was pouring water in a cup.
I listened as the sound filled the room.
Then as if gasping for air, words
tumbled from my mouth.
"I'm not going back to that house!"
My plate trembled.
The walls seemed to shake.
I'd broken Father's rule for silence
but didn't care.

A shadow crossed Mother's stern face,
her eyes reaching out.

"Never again," I asserted.
My brother Leith scuffled his feet.
My sister Edra stared.
Ears, bodies suddenly alert, Father fixed me
with his eye. "You need to return, Adah.
There's an agreement," he said.

He didn't ask my reason, a kind of grace
because I knew I didn't have the words,
wouldn't be able to say aloud the reason.

Everything about Father was a firm line:
his face, his teeth, his shirt sleeves, his jacket's edge.

He had set the ranch's fence posts that pressed
across the prairie, marking territory, defining rights.
He created rules to put everything in place
that otherwise might blend into grass
undulating with winds across the plains.

I believed he cared about me in his own way.
Didn't he sometimes call me Addey?

But now there was no bending grass.
I peered through the frosted window behind him.
Snow drifts piled high into a heavy, motionless mass
too deep to measure.

Earlier, Father read to us from Exodus
in the family Bible, the story where rivers
had turned to blood, and a locust storm so thick
it blinded the sun as they devoured Egypt's green—
I was living that story now.
Blood pounded in my ears and every tender place
inside me felt gnawed.

Survival was grim work.
Our family needed me to return.
How could I tell Father no?
I might have to wander through my own wilderness,
but wasn't going to relive
what I endured at the Hughes's house.

Though only twelve, I determined
I had to find my own promised land.

THINGS WE DON'T TALK ABOUT—
WHAT JASPER TOLD ADAH

Crawford, Nebraska, January 1901
Jasper, age 54, Adah's father

Listen daughter, we got here by the work
of our hands, by enduring whatever came.
Our family has lived nearly two centuries
on this land starting over again and again.

We don't mention what we don't like.
Say we'll do something, and we do it.
When troublesome things cry out
wanting our attention, we let them alone.
Life doesn't bring relief
when it's not to our liking.

We live with what happens.
This is how life is—sometimes cruel,
sometimes gentle. Insects don't care
about being nice. Whatever effort a farmer took
to raise their field of grain doesn't matter.
Insects want to eat. Animals get sick. They die
giving birth or die after you stayed up all night
keeping them warm so they'd survive.

Whatever goal or good anyone aims for, nothing
is all our own making.
Snow and wind are both necessary
and can be terrifying.
These are given facts.

We don't talk about these things,
but I tell you now. Talk about contradictions
changes nothing. Move on.
Whatever horrific event happened
can't matter as much as the need for food
and a roof over our heads.

SURVIVAL METHODS

Crawford, Nebraska, January 1901
Adah, age 12

Before I was born, when she was six,
my sister Rhoda died of whooping cough.
When I was eleven, my sister Shara died
from an abortion at nineteen.

Mother waded in grief, but chores
still had to be done. Leith fed the cows,
hauled wood and water. Sewing lessons
mother started for me soon as I could hold
a needle, didn't halt for illnesses or death.

Thread and needle in hand, I restitched
overalls, shirts, and dresses' torn fabric—
worked to make what we had
last a little longer.

No needle or thread could repair
what Jacob Hughes had done, though,
when he tore me.
Nothing came together after that.
Winter's frozen world moved into my bones,
numbed my senses, splintered my life,
and placed a leaden ball in my chest.
I waited for a hand to reach out to me, a voice,
but there was none. A howling storm
hidden in my mind heaved and hurled.

When I turned nine, I went to work at the Hughes's
fine house with a thick oak table, rooms with heat,
silverware, and white napkins. A relief for my
struggling parents, my payment was food.

(continued)

Bad enough telling Father I wouldn't return
to the Hugheses. To talk further about what happened
would make it worse. Families need friends.
In a small community like Crawford, people rely
on each other and their reputations.
To name what happened would pull apart
a relationship Father worked hard to establish.

I broke the alliance when I refused to return.
The good Hugheses weren't good to me.
Their son's rough hands pulling at my clothes,
his horrible scent, blood down my legs—
it wasn't I who'd broken trust.

Though I couldn't find the words to tell the story,
Mother defended my decision. But the Hughes
kept their reputation and their secret.
I couldn't change what happened.

How I longed to run into the wheat fields,
grass blades tossing above, cutting away my sorrow,
but it was winter now.

Gazing out the window at bare fields filled with snow,
I remembered the cows.
Leaving needlework behind and icy wind
pushing at my face, I trudged across thick-fallen snow
to the barn. Opening the door, an earthy scent
filled my lungs. Gold-flecked straw
drifted through the air.

"Clara," I called to my favorite cow.
She meandered forward, then stood beside me.
"Clara," I said. She looked into me with her large,
lucid eyes. Clara knew about loneliness and standing
in the shadowed cold for days and nights on end.

Putting my arm around her neck I leaned into
her warmth—a solid, gentle presence, and told her
everything as we stood there in the darkness,
tears tumbling out of some deep hole inside me
into a faint light drifting down in shafts
from high above.

Quietly, Clara listened for a long time as if she, too,
needed company. Then I walked back to the house.
Cold against cold, I turned to shut the kitchen door.

In the yard, stacked hard against poles Father
had carefully set around the house, snowdrifts
pushed through the fence wires
as if to topple them.

ADELLA'S ADVICE

Crawford, Nebraska, February 1901
Adella, age 44, Adah's mother

She couldn't say it, but I understood something too big
to talk about had happened to Adah.

Her step was heavy, as if carrying some great weight,
her eyes withdrawn, face secretive—not like

her usual self, delighting in cloud shapes, a cedar
waxwing's call, or animal print found in snow.

Her father's advice wasn't enough.
I brought her into the kitchen. It was time

to teach her how to make noodles. I put on my apron
with the embroidered yarrow flowers,

"Known for healing," my mother said when she
taught me how to stitch. I beckoned Adah beside me

and began. "First you fold the ingredients
for the noodles: flour, egg, water. A bit of salt."

Adah gazed up at me, lip trembling. I wasn't certain
what had happened to her. She wouldn't say,

and if she did, how could we talk about it?
No words describe the worst of what touches us.

The truest things in the world I understand
with my hands, my eyes.

The absent look on her face, her weighted walk,
tell me her spirit has been robbed.

Something at the house she'd worked at harmed her.
How could I find words to tell her anything to restore

what she lost when I've never found the words
for any tragedy I've known? So, I carried on

with the lesson. "Don't measure too much.
Lots of measuring, and you won't have the feel

for when you have too much of one thing
or not enough of the other. Adjust as you go.

Taste a bit of mixture you're making
to see if it seems good.

Whatever you're making, this is how to do it.
Then, let it rest. Do something else for a while."

We straightened and set things right in the kitchen,
then repaired a few holes in socks, returning afterwards

to the noodles. I looked at the dough on the counter,
a lump stuck in my throat as I described directions.

"Now, flatten it. Press it down. Roll it even
like the plains," I explained. "A solid, smooth surface,

but pliable. Think of the moment you despise,
then roll the dough flat."

I pushed the dough outward with the pin.
Adah gathered some dough and following me,

placed it in front of her. "If it's too sticky, add
some flour to help you do what you want it to.

You're the cook." Her eyes went wide. Aware.
"You understand what I'm telling you?"

(continued)

She nodded. "Pictures, smells, words, fear,
whatever's in your memory, put them

into these noodles. Look at the mixture closely,
feeling for when it's ready.

Then cut the dough in strands."
Adah took a knife and sliced the dough in strips.

"Right. Now, throw them in the boiling water.
Stir them so they don't stick together.

This is how we do it. We cook, and when we cook,
we change everything."

Two

STORM
1903–1908

WIND RISE

Crawford, Nebraska, 1903
Adella, age 46, Adah's mother

Spring was over. Summer too.
My hands were full of garden vegetables
for our supper's soup. I wanted to add in beet greens,
and had come to gather them, but put everything
down to sit on the steps at the front door
to take in the sky as I like to do.

Jasper was out working in the field, Cedric napping,
Leith, Edra, and Jamie at school. Adah stays focused
on doing laundry since not working for the Hughes,
doesn't want to return to school.
It was just me sitting there, watching clouds
lounge in the forever sky, resting long shadows
across the earth. There's a whole lot of forever
on this prairie, a world filled with space
to hold Jasper's dreams, mine,
and stow away our sorrows too.

Lenore has left home now, is cooking for folks
in Newcastle. I feel her absence, but it was Shara,
my oldest, I held in mind—her fine blue eyes
the day she left home, blue as this here sky,
and my sister's short letter come from Montana
three years ago now 'bout Shara dying up there
her baby aborted amidst fever, the bleeding,
and no way to help her survive.

Nothing could be done either for six-year-old
Rhoda the morning she gave up coughing
eighteen years ago now, her red hair bright
as polished copper as her body lay damp
and limp against the pillow.

The wind came up strong, rattled our house.
Moaned. The sky turned dark and bruised.
Clouds reeled toward the house, tall as mountains
full of gray weight, and broke open. Rain
tumbled down in great heaves, loosened
weight carried for miles.

My husband Jasper is all earth, likes rules,
and order's firm ground. I see the need,
but savor the wind's rush along my skin,
through my hair,
my clothes, how it lifts,
brings me breath,
pushes me past thought.

This evening's soup holds beets' earth-red essence.
I lift the liquid to my lips, swallow the residue
of rain and wind. I wasn't born on this land
but belong to it and its winds,
trust the life in it.

WHAT DID I KNOW?

Crawford, Nebraska, 1905
Adah, age 16

I was sixteen. What did I know of marriage?
Claude was handsome, a railroad brakeman
who'd been to Chicago, played guitar, and sang
at Crawford's barn dances when in town.

We met over biscuits I brought to the dance.
"Perfect mix of tart and sweet," he said
biting into the bready softness
spread with current jam. "Like you."

Claude controls a train's speed, makes sure
people can see the train coming.
I didn't see the direction he was headed
when our relationship turned a corner.

"Too much traveling," Mother said
when I talked about Claude.
But I wanted to leave my parents'
rigid home, and Claude's music
made me ache for something more
than the world I was born into—
created a longing that lifts above the horizon
into the forever sky where the world
becomes borderless.

I married Claude anyway
behind my parents' backs.
Learned it was true what Mother said.
Claude traveled.

The loneliness derailed me.

Why marry, then spend days alone in a bare,
rented room doing the same chores as before,
when he's off gallivanting across the countryside?

I could have put up with it if it was just that.
Maybe.
But what was the point?

We were barely married when Claude left
on the CB&Q train run up north to Montana.
Gone for weeks.

He smelled of coal fumes, wanted a good spin
in bed soon as he returned, and craved more
of my "tasty biscuits." It wasn't a marriage
for me.

"I married you because you wanted
out of your parents' house," he told me,
trying to make things sound right.

But then revealed he had a woman
in Billings too—
wanted me to be okay with it.

I am young, inexperienced, but no.
I wasn't doing that.
Straight away, I had the marriage annulled.
Don't need to consider it real.

I loved Claude for the sound of his voice,
places he'd been, and that we might go.
Yes. I chose to marry him, but see now
it's better to choose a steady man with stable work.

Once again, I'm staying with Mother and Father.
Sometimes things feel normal—I'm washing dishes,
hanging laundry, cutting noodles for soup.

A short time later I'm drifting in a haze,
the kind summer throws over the body
where a person needs to sit in the shade to recover.

(continued)

That's what I'm doing now, sitting in the shade,
watching grass blades bend when words to a song
surfaces that Claude sang, and I recall how
smoothly his fingers slid across a guitar's neck—
how practiced he was at pressing down
on the precise place to get the response he wanted.

His voice tumbles through me like water.
"Oh, hard times, hard times, come again
no more⋯" and I think of how easily
gladness can be lost inside longing's
dry, blue voice.

I want to run away,
find a different life,
but can't.

Got to learn to live the life I have.

JED PONDERS MANIFEST DESTINY

Beaver Creek, Weston, Wyoming, 1906
Jed, age 43, Adah's brother-in-law, Lenore's husband

God wanted me to have this land here in Weston.
The government affirmed it was mine
for the taking, as if God had spoken to them
like he spoke to Abraham, promising
a great nation would grow from his offspring.

I wasn't sure I understood.
Who knows God's mind?

I want to make a life off this land, but the ones
most able to do that are people like Mr. Swan
with his giant tracts of land. That gold-toothed cheat
owns most the cattle and sheep across Nebraska,
South Dakota, and Wyoming, while the rest of us
work our tails off to get by on what he pays.

Sheering sheep, planting hay, one event follows
another. Cracked leather, worn soles, encrusted
with soil, my shoes tell my story.

The land asks more of me
than I can give.

The Good Book says, "There's a way
that appears to be right, but in the end
leads to death." Farming and ranching
are the life I know, so I stick with it.
I can't think much about what's right.

People say my wife looks like an Indian, tease
about her dark hair and skin, as if her destiny
should be something else.

(continued)

Lenore's steady, determined, and works hard.
She makes mighty fine fry bread and beans,
keeps house, and manages a farm.

Most of us don't know much about the truth
of our own stories,
much less questions of destiny.

This I know: work
is my destiny.

I give myself to it.

LENORE'S WISH

Beaver Creek, Weston, Wyoming, 1907
Lenore, age 24, Adah's sister

While living at our parents' house, we children
were servants controlled with harsh words
and the back of Father's hand.

Unlike Father, my husband Jed was a quiet man.
That pleased me.
Hours working in the field each day,
he's used to the silence, too tired
to talk much, though he always comments
on my good cooking, is partial
to my chili and corncakes.

Milking sheep and caring for cattle
alongside Jed, birdsong
and the evening's calm,
this was a life I loved,
but lonely too.

While crocheting in the evening
or stitching a quilt, I longed for conversation.
Mother now had four children younger than Adah.
Jed and I asked Adah to come stay with us.
Lord knows, one less to care for or feed
would bring Mother relief.

To live in this world, a woman needs resourcefulness,
and a multitude of skills. Together Adah and I
gardened, cut cloth for quilts, cleaned and cooked.

On warm evenings sometimes we'd pull
the davenport outside to stare at stars— the faraway
dim lights in night's vast blanket containing
countless worlds beyond our comprehension.

(continued)

Violent storms with cloud-filled skies, bursting
with angry rain, bent grass wavering beneath
noon-heavy sun, animal sweat and broken earth,
insects humming, lambs' thick wool, stained
and thread-bare clothes, coal embers for irons,
buckets filled with water from the well and carried
a quarter mile, freshly washed clothes fluttering
on the line, the comfort of hot biscuits, hungry days,
lonely blue nights, and cows' low moans—

the history of all that came before us,
those whose feet had touched the earth
we labored over—
this was the world we understood.
Adah and I were made of these.

I wished for Adah's grief to be like chaff
carried by wind, for her to be able to tell the story,
words transforming the pain, blowing away
despair's debris.

As with everyone else we knew, only one place
felt safe for Adah—one that stitched closed
sorrow's night-filled pockets.

Together we leaned into each other like stars—
distant bodies held together by gravity,
and light's ephemeral bridges between
the gigantic gaps and pin-pricked brightnesses
creating the constellations that shaped our lives.

HOW WINTER ARRIVED

Beaver Creek, Weston, Wyoming, 1908
Jed, age 45, Adah's brother-in-law, Lenore's husband

It wasn't anything expected, the ferocity
of that winter's night, the way the cold

seeped into the bones like a fierce fire
shaking the foundations of the house.

There wasn't enough coal or blankets
to temper or soothe the body into sleep.

"Come with us," Lenore called to Adah.
Cautiously, she climbed beneath our blanket,
and the three of us hunkered there against
the rage outside.

We'd never been close this way.
First my arm around Lenore,
her arm around Adah. Then our legs.
       Then my arms around
             the two of them,
then my hands on their breasts, heft of hip,
I slipped beyond the border, pulled clothing
       loose, unraveled with the howling wind
    as it hurled against the house, bit at the boards,
shook the bed and thrashed against the door.

Clouds pelted snow sideways, thrust flakes
       into mounding drifts, sloping into
ice-carved edges. Wind
whirling outside, hair loose,
and limbs, bodies rolled and turned on the bed.

Any line that before created a boundary
between the territories of what was right
I pushed through.

                         (continued)

Though they tried to push me away,
though they cried, I took the women,
both of them.
Any thought
I was a peaceful man

gone.

ADAH MAKES A QUILT WITH LENORE

Beaver Creek, Weston, Wyoming, 1908
Lenore, age 25, Adah's sister

The storm passed.
Adah and I lay on the bed holding each other.
First sobbing.   Then still.

Still as the holes in a night sky.
Stillness so deep
it felt audible.

No breath of wind outside.
No birds calling, moon-glaze,
or crackled fall from an icicle's sudden break.
Only snow's cover stifling all.

Silently, Adah put on her clothes, her coat,
took a blanket, left without a word,
and headed for the barn.

Pushing Jed to the floor,
I turned to face the wall.
There was no changing what happened.

In the morning, I opened the cabin's door.
The prairie's expansive waste of colorless white
mirrored my spirit's emptiness.

The world I thought I was living in
I no longer inhabited.

My eyes wandered the horizon's low line.
I thought of the Lakota who belonged to this land
before we arrived, grief's whispers, immense
as the plains rising from the earth tumbled through me
like the windstorm endured last night, a spinning squall
that would never die down.

(continued)

My stomach crimped into a knot.
The sky was clear but felt as if it were filled
with smoky haze.

Life would be different now.

Jed left for the field.
I went to the barn to find Adah curled beside the cows.
I knelt beside her, reaching for her hand.
She let me hold it.

For a long time, we said nothing,
just let the tears roll down—a shared mercy.

I'm a strong woman,
but couldn't keep Jed from Adah,
though I tried.

Like a great wave, shame washed over me,
sadness filling me with an immense weight.

"I'm sorry," I said, holding her gaze steadily.
Knowingly, she looked at me and nodded,
her eyes deep pools.

Later, we went inside. We made a bowl
of noodle soup, then took last night's torn clothing
and cut them into pieces for a quilt.

Gathering blocks cut previously
and adding them to those newly made,
piece by piece, we laid out a design.

Then, threading needles, we began to sew,
the two of us piecing together,
as women do,
some semblance of comfort
from the patchwork fabric
into which everything unravels.

JED GOES FOR A WALK

Beaver Creek, Weston, Wyoming, 1908
Jed, age 45, Adah's brother-in-law, Lenore's husband

When Lenore shoved me from the bed,
I went to the fields. The depth of the snow
or direction I went—none of that mattered.

I wasn't sure where I was going anyway.

True, it was fiercely cold and there weren't
blankets enough to keep warm, but when Lenore
invited Adah into bed with us, what was I to think?

For me it wasn't about keeping warm.
After two years of marriage,
Lenore hadn't gotten pregnant.
Even if a burden to provide for,
a child could be a help.
Especially if it were a boy.

Truthfully, I wasn't thinking about that last night,
or thinking about Adah either.

I'm more than twenty years older than Lenore.
I've laid with women often enough before marriage
to know more than one woman in bed is a gift.

Even when Lenore tried pushing me
from Adah—two women beside me in bed,
the naked shock of their smoothness,
the ecstasy of standing inside a river's rush,
hands full of their round flesh—
I couldn't think.
Only wanted their silken fullness
sliding over me.

It wasn't about love or beauty,
or who means what to who.   *(continued)*

It was as if God had spoken:
I had to be satisfied.

I knew then
what I was capable of
even if I didn't want to be that man.

I didn't know if Lenore would ever
invite me back to bed.
Didn't want to face living
with Adah in the house either.

"Listen to the light within," Mother used to say
when I was faced with struggles.
Problem is, after leaving Pennsylvania,
I hadn't listened for years.

Again, the words come back to me:
"There's a way that appears to be right,
but in the end leads to death."
Guess that's true of any relationship.

Lenore's strong, determined. I wanted
a new life when I married her, want her now
despite the mess I've made.

Women have legal rights, can own
their own property and businesses.
Lenore could leave me,
work as she did before as a cook.

But I doubt she'd choose that.
Neither would she or Adah go to court
to make public a story
about what happened in bed.
It'd only shame them,
make their chance for work worse.

The seams on the welt of one of my boots
came loose. A wet-cold seeped in through the sole.

I turned to head home.

I'll be okay. Things'll work out.
I might not be a good man.
But I can trust in Lenore's goodness.

AS WE ARE

Beaver Creek, Weston, Wyoming, 1908
Lenore, age 25, Adah's sister

How could I love myself
      when what I held precious
      has crumbled into dry earth,
      my body a winter's desert
      the weight of stone.

How could I lift my life
      beyond what had shamed me
      when grief had left a scar
      I didn't know how to heal?

I made Adah a private space at the house
      with solid walls
      where she didn't need to see
      or speak to Jed,
      had room
      to re-create herself.

I baked her muffins, and brought her
      grilled lamb, and fresh trout
      from the creek when I could.

My mother found a way to love
      Father's hard heart,
      but I stay away from Jed.
      I'm not sure how to set things
      straight, but make certain
      he stays away from Adah too.

Memory circles like a ceaseless wind
      without escape. While I wash dishes,
      I wipe a cloth over and over the rings
      of sorrow, relive what went wrong,
      wishing to erase what happened.

I don't know how to live into the days ahead,
      but this evening when Jed walked in
      after shoveling snow and feeding cattle.
      I looked at his earth-brown eyes,
      wind-chapped hands, work-worn shoes,
      quiet shoulders—and remembered
      we are people of earth.

      Ashes are food for fruit and roses,
      not merely the sight of a tree's death.
      Seeds find ways into stone's cracks
      and grow.

      Failures and their consequences
      have their season.

      Brokenness brings humility.
      But it's not the end.

Love is deeper than grief.
      We're more than the torn fabric
      of our mistakes and histories,
      more than our skin and scars.

DAYDREAMING WITH CLOUDS

Beaver Creek, Weston, Wyoming, 1908
Adah, age 19

Nineteen years old and pregnant.
No. I didn't want this to happen to me.

My life had barely begun before it was over.
In the world I was born into, a girl became
a cleaner, cook, teacher, nurse, wife, mother,
or a prostitute. The possibilities were few
and already determined.

But between permitted roles
lay hidden skills and hopes.

Women I knew harnessed and trained horses,
managed farms and budgets, repaired fences,
and used hammers, rakes and hoes.
They planted, harvested, canned,
and knew how to heal animals.

I wore baggy dresses to cover my growing belly,
remained as invisible in public as possible
to ensure I could still have a future
with some potential worth waiting for.

Yes, I was expecting—expecting to be more
than what someone thought of me, more than
the wretched things I experienced, different
from what I was told I could be,
was expected to be, or the tedious job
someone assigned me.

Hanging clothes to dry after laundry, I imagined
lives walking around inside the clothes
different from those who usually wore them.

My parents' house was full of shouts and icy silence.
Picturing a life beyond what I'd lived was difficult.
If I could choose what I want to do, I'd grow a garden
full of flowers and bring bouquets to pregnant women
and to women who lean over laundry tubs all day,
scrubbing away dirt.

I wasn't a normal girl.

If I could choose, I'd have a shop selling flowers
and linens. My family made fun of my love
for napkins and tablecloths when I put them
on the table for ranch hands to use
who likely cared little for niceties.
But why must a person be rich to appreciate
being given something beautiful?

Waiting for a birth I never wished for
while sitting at my sister's window, I daydreamed
of meadows filled with blue flax, violets, primroses,
mountain lilies, and yarrow. Clouds shifted shape,
parts of them dissolving,   disappearing,
then moving on.

If the voiceless cries inside could be made visible,
I'd turn them into flowers, scatter petals
everywhere. Flowers' fragrance and beauty
wash through a room softly, the way birds' wings
trail through sky, the way rain's gentleness
rinses the world in spring.

Stark, colorless rooms full of calloused hearts
and soured lives, I'd seen enough ugliness in life—
people need beauty
as much as they need breath.

Three

Drought
1908

DURING DROUGHT

Beaver Creek, Weston, Wyoming, 1908
Adah, age 19

Earth crackled underfoot, hot winds
peeled the skin, crops shriveled
and collapsed, banks floundered,
farmers sold their livestock.

Some lost their farms, others their homes.
Then, on the brink of famine at the end
of a decade of drought,
I was born.

The ghosts of the world that came before
and what was coming next
rose from the soil to the fever-weary air.

Parched earth's despair eventually passed,
but a new drought arrived when I got pregnant.
Barely past childhood,
I was living in one world,

then woke to realize
I was living in another.

Arid wind evaporated my life,
withered thoughts of any restful future.

Heat exhausts.
Lack of water alters the mind.
We need rain, streams, lakes.
We need rivers' soft arms to hold us.

I understood little about anything.
Except thirst.

So, I went to the fields and meadows,
days and months walking alone
through wave-thick grass, green and gold pastures
under gentle skies strewn with clouds.

Flowing forth as if a spring, crested penstemon
and desert buckbean grew out of cracks in rocks.

Shadows shifting and lifting in crests across the prairie,
I journeyed into fields, the earth's wordless voice
entering slowly through my feet and eyes,
seeping through the silence, whispering within
the perseverance of its expansive presence
that I was more than the hurt and harm I felt,
larger than what had happened to me,
and that like the earth, I, too,
would find a way to endure.

CONSIDERING WHAT HAPPENED

Beaver Creek, Weston, Wyoming, 1908
Jed, age 45, Adah's brother-in-law, Lenore's husband

"When is this baby going to come?"
Adah repeated the question so often
it became a plea. Back aching, body heavy,
she crawled across the floor on all fours,
begged for release.
She'd stayed at home, avoided dances,
trips to town, kept her body secret.

I watched her belly increase week by week,
heard her groans. Guilt gnawed at my chest.
As her body expanded with the growing baby,
so did the weight of what I'd done.
I wanted to look away, but living with her discomfort
made what I did to her impossible to ignore.
I'd betrayed Lenore, harmed her and Adah.
I'd created that misery, wasn't free from it.

"The shame isn't Adah's," Lenore said.
"How are we going to live together now?"

There's a fierceness in Lenore.
She knows how to cope with hardness.
I see it in her knife's deftness
when she cuts flesh from bone for soup,
notice it as she pierces through winter's ice.
Her resolve cuts into me.

I couldn't remain as I was.
I needed her kindness, her grace.

Wind blew across the plains,
hurled through the tablelands, pushed
into my ears, my bones,
stripped me down.
Emptied me.

COMING TO TERMS

Beaver Creek, Weston, Wyoming, 1908
Lenore, age 25, Adah's sister

Adah was adamant. She'd not have an abortion
like her sister Shara who'd traveled all the way
to Billings to have it done, only to get an infection
and bleed to death afterwards.

"Adah has no home now," I told Jed.

I know how to cook, but my husband has skills
with tools, and animals. He can read their personalities
and needs. He can round up and move cows, get sheep
to change direction. Rounding up his wandering mind,
living with his failures' knotted consequences
was far more difficult.

For both of us.

Shoulders slumped, feet dragging, Jed
walked through the house as if plowing
a field of stone. Though he'd not considered
any consequences the night he got Adah pregnant,
it was clear something had to be done
to help Adah.

He didn't know how to be a father.
We decided anyway.
No other way we could live together.

Out of my love for Adah,
and his need for forgiveness—
we agreed to adopt Adah's child,
raise it as our own, carry that weight
the rest of our lives.

(continued)

We described our decision to Adah.
Relieved, she agreed. It seemed reasonable
and right.

"But nothing about this," she said,
"can ever be fair."

We remained silent.
She left the room.

Jed went to the yard to repair a fence.
I stood at the door looking out to where he worked,
then past to the horizon's far edge.

Out there on that wind-scrubbed earth
has he ever heard the voice of grass he walks on?

Has he considered what more Adah and I
might long for, what we understand
that he has never imagined?

ADELLA ASSISTS ADAH GIVING BIRTH

Beaver Creek, Weston, Wyoming, 1908
Adella, age 51, Adah's mother

Lenore boiled water. I put on my embroidered apron,
laid out clean cloth pads.

Adah didn't want this baby. "Why'd he do this to me?"
she cried out, convulsed with pain. Contractions
grabbed and drug her into their undertow,
crested and broke through her body.
"I'm going to die!" she howled.
"You're my daughter.
Bear it and breathe," I told her.

Lenore placed a damp cloth on her forehead.
"This won't last forever," she said.

Body stretched to the excruciating edge of endurance,
after nine hours of teeth gnashing and gripping cramps,
the baby was born.
Exhausted, Adah held the child to her breast,
candlelight illuminating her body.

The rest of the room filled with darkness.
From the womb's darkness   into a wider darkness,
this is the way we arrive in the world.
So little we understand. Nothing is certain.

Every birth brings piercing pain and blood.
In every moment we both live and die.

I've borne the prairie's pummeling
for years. So will Adah.
She knows more of the strength
she's made of now.

Lenore and Adah have chosen the child's name—
Margot, the pearl.

KNOTS

Beaver Creek, Weston, Wyoming, 1908
Adah, age 19

Jed was good with ropes.
In the evening, he'd practice tying knots.
He had knots for everything: slip knots
to tighten a hold on things so they couldn't
fall out but he could still readily undo
the knot when he wanted,

a cinch knot for holding things down
or in, a square knot for tying together
two ropes when he didn't want things
to easily loosen—like the stories
he didn't want to get out.

Like the truth about what happened in bed
that winter night nine months ago
the way things slipped loose.
The knot he tied in me then, the rope
of his child growing inside me.

The cinch knot of the girl's life I gave him,
the square knot I tied with my sister who
took that girl to raise her with Jed as their own.

He used to sit in the living room's dark
after the baby was born, saying nothing.

He had turned to carving by then.
He'd carve shape after shape,
then toss it into the fire,
watch it burn.

Over and over.

As if he had never once
tied a knot in his life.

THE BLUE DRESS

Beaver Creek, Weston, Wyoming, 1908
Adah, age 19

After her birth, I nursed Margot for a time,
but the girl was to be Lenore and Jed's.
Not mine.

I needed to leave their house, wanted work,
but not in the fields like my sister Edra
who enjoyed ranch life.
I wasn't interested in a life of sweat
and calloused hands.

I wanted the respect marriage gives a woman,
but wasn't considered a good woman
since Jed had gotten me pregnant.
I had ideas about what good means,
but had to keep those thoughts to myself.

Longing for something to bolster my spirits
and give me strength, I dared to dream of a dress,
an astonishing dress that could carry me
into a different life, one with a smooth texture
where I could feel alive, new,
and I sketched a picture.

When supply wagons came to town,
I found and bought the ideal fabric.

A superb seamstress, Lenore created the pattern
and sewed the dress—blue cotton, the color of rivers.

The fabric flowed from my waist like a stream
over a meadow, tasteful, but gorgeous
with polished buttons.
It fit perfectly.

(continued)

Sheridan was expanding quickly.
Maids were sure to be wanted in Sheridan.
In my new blue dress, I believed I could become
a woman with more than one dress
and one pair of shoes.

In my wonderful blue dress, the color
of my birthstone, I could ride a fine horse,
choose between foods I'd prefer to eat,
own property perhaps. I'd have to marry,
but I could run a business, sell fine fabrics
to women in any shade they pleased.

I believed that in Sheridan it'd be possible
to rise into a spacious blue beyond the clay-hard earth
of what was expected of me.

Four

Edges
1908–1915

BEGINNING NEW

Beaver Creek, Weston, Wyoming, 1908
Jed, age 45, Adah's brother-in-law, Lenore's husband

Adah left.
We were alone with Margot now.
Lenore cradled the baby in her arms
as I stared into her small face.

Her hand reached toward me.
I held out a finger and she latched on.
"Hold her," Lenore suggested.

What if I dropped her?
I understood how to fix tools
and prepare for bad weather.
But raising a child
scared me.

Lenore thrust Margot into my arms anyway.
That little scamp curled into me
as if I was some kind of blanket.
She didn't know I was broken.

Light fell through the window
onto Margot's open face.
I felt her weight and fell silent.

The responsibility expanded in my mind—
the time,
effort,
cost.

Some fathers would be more experienced, wise.

Didn't matter.
I was her father now,
had to begin anyway.

WHEN ADAH MET GERARD

Sheridan, Wyoming, 1909
Adah, age 20

Gerard was painting down the hall from where I
was cleaning the room where Buffalo Bill used to stay

when he lived at Sheridan's Inn. Gerard showed me
the room he was completing, pointed out how walls

of Prussian blue reverberated in the light, the shaded
variations where corners met. He was different

from other men. Listening to his voice's rich depth,
I felt his warmth radiate through the room.

He experienced color the way I did when I walked
through late summer's fields, birds calling overhead,

grass rippling, insects throbbing, as clouds blended
into other clouds, and the shadows of clouds.

As he prepared the paint color for the next room,
he described how he could match a wall to the color

of sage, feathers from a mountain bluebird,
or ripe wheat. In his presence I felt relaxed,

comfortable. I met him again that weekend
at a local dance. The band played "Beautiful Isle

of Somewhere," and "I'm Glad I Met You."
Unlike me, Gerard knew the popular songs

and made me laugh as he sang along.
A big personality with dreams, he described

(continued)

his hopes to own a house, see more of the countryside,
and to paint as many major buildings as he could.

He told me I had courage and determination,
thought I was an uncommon girl.

Such words tasted sweeter than cake.
I wanted to be with him.

It was as if I'd been living in a desert
then stepped into a glorious garden.

No one had ever told me such things.
Like wild iris opening their deep throats

or blazing stars bursting with bright tendrils,
this was what love felt like, I told myself.

He had steady work,
would be here a while I thought,

and I cracked open
my heart's lock.

GERARD'S ABSENCE

Sheridan, Wyoming, 1909
Adah, age 20

I'd been seeing Gerard only briefly in Sheridan
before he left for Iowa to attend to his ill mother,
I didn't know how long he'd be gone. But I stayed put.

Much bigger than Crawford where I was born,
in Sheridan people spoke languages I'd never heard,
and a sweet scent from the candy kitchen drifted
down Main Street. The Inn had coal-powered lights
where years earlier Buffalo Bill's performers
entertained guests with his Wild West show.

Men came to Sheridan from around the world
to mine coal, mill sugar and flour, brew beer,
or raise horses for polo teams, though I
never saw a game.

I cleaned rooms and served food at thick oak tables
with tablecloths and crisp, white napkins.
It was a new life.

Sometimes on certain afternoons, the sun
fell through windows setting aglow
the tables' water glasses.
As if a bubbling spring, the room hummed
and murmured in conversation—
people setting up plans, closing deals.

Subtle *tings* played against plates and bowls
as people ate, creating a kind of music.
The room shimmered the way morning's dew
quivers on grass strands before a droplet falls.
For a few moments the world flowed as if in dance.

Through the window the world opened
in an enormous sweep of boundless earth.
I was far from the world I was born into
and glad of it.

OBSERVATIONS

Sheridan, Wyoming, 1909
Adah, age 20

I loved the buzz of Sheridan's streets, the gleam
from electric lamps at night.

At work, I overheard businessmen making deals,
and became familiar with the women
who worked there and regularly
helped seal those deals.

Sometimes in the Inn's hallway, the women
brushed by in low-cut dresses of sumptuous silk
decorated with lace or sequins, a luscious rustle
in their skirts as they accompanied men
to their rooms—mustached middle-aged men
wearing polished leather shoes, older men,
cane in hand, or men my own age in fine felt hats.

I was taught to keep my body private, to never talk
about what men and women did behind closed doors.

From these women I heard histories like mine
of men who'd stolen their dreams. From them
I learned how to ensure having a child
would be my choice.

Some of these same women gave money to schools
and churches, worked to improve the town.

I didn't want to sell my body, but understood
the desire and need. Skin touching skin.
A few minutes of pleasure, craving fulfilled—
people rub against each other, but rarely
are we ever truly touched or understood.

Who is innocent or guilty grows cloudy
when everyone's stories are tied together.

THE EDGE OF A NEW BEGINNING

Sheridan, Wyoming, 1909
Adah, age 20

Gerard's mother recovered, and he returned to Sheridan
in winter, wanting to see me. I didn't want to continue
renting a room from people Jed knew.

Perhaps I should've waited longer to learn Gerard's
moods, his ways. But Gerard had good skills,
was handsome. Most of all, he wanted me.

I didn't want to remain alone. So, on a chilly morning,
wind reaching toward the Big Horn mountains,
then rising through crisps of cloud

inside a cavernous sky, I married Gerard at Holy Name
Catholic Church. I knew little about Catholics,
but liked the way they kept Jesus on a cross

as if they knew suffering continues even when you're
not looking directly at it, how pain changes
the way a person sees everything.

I liked how incense filled the church, as if the world
could still be sweet with possibility, even though
I might feel empty, and paper dry.

I liked how lit candles became prayers, a recognition
that the deepest prayers don't have words.
I loved thinking of Mary as merciful—

a mother to call on when I needed hope. I longed
for mercy, yearned for its sweetness.
When I could find none adequate,

the rosary gave me words to confess my grief—
the sorrow that had seeped into my body
like flood water to hold me under   *(continued)*

when I wanted, instead, to look up at stars,
hear them singing into the silence
like cicadas throbbing

with light. So, casting fear aside, on December eighth
I made confession and pledged my troth.
For better or worse, I married Gerard,

then waded deep into his arms until daylight subsided
into twilight's hovering darkness and we
surfaced to the waning moon

and thin air.

CARVING

Beaver Creek, Weston, Wyoming, 1910
Jed, age 47, Adah's brother-in-law, Lenore's husband

"Fresh eggs! Cook 'em in a pot, cook 'em in a pan,
fresh eggs, get 'em while you can." A peddler,
my father sold groceries from his carriage—
beans, carrots, butter, and eggs. All day
he sang out describing his produce to passersby,
voice echoing through the neighborhoods
as he walked his horses down Reading's streets.

At the day's end of chanting, he loved returning home
to sit in silence. "God speaks when you listen,"
he told me as we walked beneath ruby-leafed maples
when I was thirty, me wondering about
leaving Pennsylvania, moving west.

I'd worked with him for years but was never good
at selling. "Trees understand seasons," he said
lifting his head to the fiery boughs. "They speak
through their leaves, recognize when it's time
to let go," his voice gentle as wind amongst maples
as he turned toward me.

I left Pennsylvania with his blessing, wandered my way
toward Wyoming. Was years before I met Lenore
at the restaurant in Newcastle. Came by every week
for her smile and a bite of pie.

Lenore ignored imperfections, made people feel
comfortable. Never mentioned my shyness, age,
or the mole on the side of my face.

It was summer. No trees changing color,
but I felt as if leaves inside me had turned
bright and fell. The ground burned with light
everywhere I walked.

(continued)

Lenore is more than twenty years younger,
but I was ready to put away my lonely ways,
change my life when we met.
She believed we could grow old together,
and we married, moved north.

During the day I work on Swan's ranch—
check fences, haul hay, shovel manure.
I've shoveled a lot of dung in my time.
But now I've got to shovel myself out
from the muck I've told myself
about what a man needs—my right to take
what I want. Yes. I've been that man.
Am worse for it too.

I want Lenore's love, want to walk and work
together with her into our white-haired years.
But there's no softness in her eyes these days.
No warmth or apple pies.
She barely speaks to me now,
doesn't come near. I've trampled
her trust.

I may be mostly blind, but I see my need
to change. There is no excuse
for how I took Adah. No apology
adequate either. What I did was wrong.
Words aren't enough.
Horses and cows kick when mistreated.
Water a plant and it grows.
People are no different.
I've got to give what I want in return.
That's how it works.

Integrity, equality—my parents taught me these
when a boy. It's a Quaker's way.
Could use their help to teach me how to grow
humble, but they're gone and I'm old now.
Got to teach myself, so I've taken up carving.

Whittling's quiet work, and slow.
Each evening, branch in hand, I take my knife,
and carve, thinking about those parts of me
I could cut away: my need to have the first
plate of food and the largest, the requirement
that my opinions about weather, politics,
or someone's behavior are correct.
My insistence that Lenore meet me in bed.

I carve each piece then toss it in the fire.
Long shapes and smooth. Short forms
and blunt. Sometimes I carve the same shape
ten, twenty times. Learning is slow.

One by one, night after day, into the flames
they go, each petty pronouncement
and selfish insistence.
"To hell with them all," I say,
then lean in, listen closely
for any whispers of a turning
inside the fire that might transform me.

BARN DANCE WITH THE FAMILY

Chugwater, Wyoming, 1910
Avery, age 17, Adah's brother

Adah and Gerard stopped off on their way to Des Moines,
Edra came down from Wheatland, along with scores
of others from across the countryside riding in on horses
to Chugwater. Families pulled up in their wagons, filling
the barn, ready to dance all night and into the morning.

People brought their instruments inviting us
to join in singing to new songs like "He's My Pal,"
and "By the Light of the Silvery Moon."

Cedric and Leith are laughing. Edra and Jamie
gulp root beer while Adah nibbles on potato salad.
We weren't harvesting or herding, planting,
cooking, or cleaning. We were there for forgetting
and for joy, for music, and for each other.

My family knows I'm not good at difficult tasks,
but I can dance. Put me on the dance floor
and my feet light a fire. No fingers point
telling me what I've done wrong.
The caller announces the moves,
and the way I move is fine with everyone.

The bass keeps rhythm as guitars strum in harmony
while the mouth harp whines and moans
and spoons keep beat. Banjo players' fingers
fly like bird wings and I soar, my feet
slipping back and forth across the floor.

A fiddler's bow races up the scale, transports
the crowd, spinning and sliding into a world
of dizzy motion. The guitarist strums out
"We Shall Rise." Humming along, I find
an empty bench to stretch out on for a rest,

"On that resurrection morning when death's
prison bars are broken, we shall rise,"
the last words I hear before drifting off to sleep.

SPEAKING OF DESIRE

Des Moines, Iowa, 1911
Adah, age 22

Gerard and I have moved to Des Moines.
His father wanted help at his carpenter shop,
and Gerard is learning to make cabinets,
practical and sturdy ones with attractive facings.
An additional skill is always useful.

Like my father, Gerard's father is a religious man
with a firm voice and demanding expectations.
Unlike my father, he is kind,
likes to sing while working.

As before marriage when living at Lenore and Jed's,
I keep house, wash clothes, and cook—sauerkraut,
and sausages, and Grumbeerkiechle—savory foods
Gerard's mother has taught me to prepare.

There's a lot I don't understand about relationships
and living with a man, but I do know I want
to be more than simply useful to Gerard,
more than a helpful assistant, chosen because
I happen to be there, the way a paintbrush
or tape measure might be selected
for a needed task.

I want to be valuable.
Not for what I can do
or who I remind him of:
his sister who shares my same name,
his first wife who died in childbirth
together with her child,
a woman he joins in bed,
or some role I fill—
but for myself.

Gerard works at the shop all day.
Evenings he labors at the desk over
the books he keeps for his father's business.

We both work long hours.

Setting work aside to wander down a road,
hoping to discover something unexpected—
that is what I long for. A spring afternoon
beside the river, our voices mingled
with water and a purple finch's warble,
or us walking under a cottonwood's leaf-flame
burning into a cloudless sky—these
are what I wish for—life
full with possibility,
open like the plains.

I want Gerard to reach for my hand,
gather me to him in a smile that says
I matter more than the role given me, more
than all the rules about clean houses in paradise,
ledgers between us balanced.

Complete.

DECISION

Crawford, Nebraska, 1914
Cedric, age 15, Adah's brother

"I'm done with ranch life," Leith said.
"Too many blizzards, dead animals.
Loss. It's never going anywhere.
I want to be a teacher."

Leith liked to read, liked to question things too,
craved conversation about books, wondered why
certain things were missing from their pages.
He wanted to leave working in the fields,
become a teacher.

But Father would have none of it.
As if a stampede of a thousand hooves
rushed through the house trampling all,
the room rumbled and quaked
with Father's voice.

Knife flashing, breath tattered, Father flung open
the family Bible's cover and cut Leith's name
from the page of births in a fury.

My heartbeat pulsed in my ear.
My sisters sobbed.

"Teaching is a woman's job. You won't survive
on a teacher's salary," Father shouted.

We'd worked for Mr. Swan or his type
for years, and where'd it gotten us?
I doubt Mr. Swan made an honest dollar
in his life. His multi-million-dollar company
cooked their books like that man Frewen did,
running his cattle around a hill three times
to trick buyers into paying for more cattle
than existed. Swan swindles people.

He and his ilk, like Mr. Whitlock, claimed
other ranchers' cattle as his own, cheated
good men like Robert Hobbs out of his entire herd.

Story goes, when Mr. Swan with his hard-pointed
eyes and gold-filled teeth used to come to Cheyenne,
along with big money bankers and cattlemen,
people cleared the way for him as if for a prince,
then hovered around, hoping to shake his hand
before he headed off to a hotel.

The year Leith was born, Swan lost a quarter
of his herd in the Big-Die up.
If you want your cattle to survive months
of freeze, you've got to give them fodder.

Nothing but sheep on Swan's ranches now.
Work for Swan, and it's illegal to run your
own cattle or horses on the range.
Gone the invitations to a meal for helping
ranchers round up animals.
Big ranchers distrust the small ones,
think they're stealing their steer,
despise homesteaders, too, for taking land
they could use for grazing their huge herds.

Leith was done working for Swan or any like him,
was interested in books and ideas, wanted
to move out. Marry.
The effort to eke out a living
wasn't going to get any easier.
Couldn't see how working as a teacher
would make him any poorer.

But Father was sixty-six. Farming and ranching
held his life. He saw no other means for survival.
Nobody was going to tell him different.

(continued)

Finished cutting, Father pulled
the portion of paper with Leith's name
from the Bible, lit a match,
and burned it.

As if walking through deep snow,
an enormous hush filled the room.

The biggest turning moments
sometimes occur in silence.
Leith's moment had occurred earlier.
Now my moment had arrived.

Too many lives plowed through living this way.
I understood how equations worked,
added things up for myself and decided.
I, too, would choose a different direction.

OUR STARTING DESTINATION

Platte River, Nebraska, 1915
Gerard, age 30, Adah's husband

Early September's golden sun expanded across
the open earth
        and wind rippled through ancient cottonwoods
the day Adah and I left my parents' home
in Des Moines.

A supply base for Europe's War, business in Cheyenne
was expanding, and I planned to buy property.
We collected our clothes, packed a few blankets,
        then turned our faces from our empty rooms.
                I had two skills now, painting
                and carpentry.
I believed life in Cheyenne would make us new.

As the train came along the Platte River near dusk,
        an enormous flock of starlings
swarmed above us, a great ever-changing
fluid shadow rotating inside the sapphire light, rising
    then lunging and dipping in unity, merging,
        then dividing,
a portion falling away
rejoining others again moments later.

We'd traveled all day, one landscape blending
into another, but for this sight we pressed our faces
to the windows, riveted to the enormous mass
        of revolving shapes as we watched their fluid
forms break apart
        then heal closed, each bird responding
to the movement of others, their thousand
restless wings
        creating together a soaring, swirling
constellation.

(continued)

A momentary pause before
plunging in a new direction, like the starlings, we too
were in movement as the train rolled across
the landscape, sliding with the wave of the world into
a new dance—floating in accord with the wind of war.

We weren't sure where our movement would lead
beyond the city where we hoped to arrive,
but wind in rustling wings gave shape to the air
as if it were a voice.

Five

CLOUDS
1916–1918

WHY EDRA MARRIED AUGUST

Wheatland, Wyoming, 1916
Edra, age 21, Adah's sister

It wasn't because Wyoming had so few women
and therefore August had fewer choices for a wife.

It wasn't because I affirmed married women's right
to keep their own wages or hold property in their

own names. Neither of us had property or much money.
He and I worked together at Two-Bar Ranch, both of us

riding horses, mending fences, milking, rounding up
sheep, caring for sick ones. I married him because

I'd met a man who wanted me to be myself, a woman
who loved horses, ranching, and working outdoors.

I moved stock, hauled hay, rode horses.
This was the life I knew, and I never wanted

to be done with it. August saw how I worked
hard, knew I could be a partner, and didn't

for an instant believe women had weak bodies.
It didn't matter he was ten years older or short

and just as poor as me. "My legs reach the ground
just like any other man's," he said.

I knew that was good ground to stand on.
August chose me as I chose him.

My mother was a teacher, knew a woman's need
for choice, the benefit it could bring,

though Father questioned her right to vote, didn't
want her "mingling with the tramps at the poll."

Mother remembered the windstorm Louisa Swain
from Laramie caused when at age seventy she became
America's first woman to vote.

Mother told me about Cheyenne's Mrs. Jenkins, too,
who didn't give an ounce of weight to the idea

that women who birthed children couldn't
carry out laws. These women were before my time

but helped make it possible for man to marry a woman,
not the idea of what a woman should be.

GERARD'S NEW BUSINESS

Cheyenne, Wyoming, 1917
Gerard, age 32, Adah's husband

I'm partial to blue,
a river or lake's liquid stretch,
      the way blue can wash calmly over skin, ripple
      through the body.
Cold blue, and hot blue flame.
          Blue rising like an eye opening
          to cerulean sky.

A blue-collar worker,
I'm a member of the painters and decorators' union
      creating my own blue dream.

Blue fabric hides grime, but we painters
wear white, not blue.
      You can't hide the paint
      that decorates our clothes.

Proud of our work, it's visible for all
to see on public buildings,
      in offices and schools,
      stores, hotels, and libraries,
though our names never appear there.

My painting business in Cheyenne has opened
at a good time. I'm reaching for the big contracts.
      Blue walls at the Plains Inn,
      blue at Fort Russell.
I paint the ceiling blue at a rich man's house,
but I'm not blue about his wealth.

Blue-handled brush in my hand,
room by room, week by week, my business grows.
I work humming the blues. It's easy
to love the blues
      when the blues
are good to you.

CONFESSION

Cheyenne, Wyoming, 1917
Adah, age 28

I confess I don't know much about tenderness
or how to have a relationship, never had gentleness
shown me growing up.

Marriage to Gerard wasn't as smooth
as I'd hoped, though his work was steady,
and I was grateful.

His moods ran through the palate of color
from lake-calm blue on holidays, to yellow delight
over catching a fish, and vivid red over a spilled
paint bucket. But he came home every day
and held me close every night.

I'm not like my sisters Edra and Jamie
who love to ride horses and work outside.
Neither am I as good a cook or creative as Lenore.

People call me pushy, petty, and stingy.
I confess I'm not what others want me to be.
But I'm not all I want to be either. It's true,
I'm tight-fisted and stubborn
about not losing even the least bit of life
I've worked hard to hold on to.

This may not be a proper confession,
but I'm telling the truth:
my heart is laid low.

I wish I knew how to break open the walls
I've built against myself—to be bigger
than an impatient, exacting woman.

Cleaning, cooking. I perform these repetitive chores,
but plead for a life greater than one of tedious tasks
the rest of my days. *(continued)*

Lord have mercy.
Absolve me.

Let no more wrongs
be done against me.

A FINAL RECOGNITION

Chugwater, Wyoming, 1917
Jasper, age 70, Adah's father

Life is labor. I round up and feed animals,
clean barns, spread manure, plow, water,
cut, stack, and bale hay, pitch sheaves,
and thresh grain. This is the effort
that has been my life.

A season of drought, the grass cattle feed on
dies, and the cattle die too.
Winters with little rain, then blizzards.
Sheep perish by the tens of thousands.

Everyone has to lose things.
But in Nebraska and Wyoming we've relived
plagues a dozen times.
I rent now, don't own a house
as I did in Nebraska.

Since people fenced the land to define
what's theirs, animals lack free range
for open eating. Ranchers have to grow
their own feed. Fences, feed—it all
costs money, ownership a dream
only the few can afford.
I've lost that dream.

Fences decreased the land's value.
The result is we've diminished ourselves.
Maybe no dream ever carries a man all the way
to the end of where he hopes to go.

Has my life's effort been for nothing
other than to labor, then die like grass
under the sun's heavy heat?

(continued)

The measure of my life, any life,
must be more than tasks accomplished,
what is lost or given up.

Adella and I've had two children die.
I needed Leith's help at the homestead
but didn't have it after he left.
I let go the Nebraska farm.
Swan's Wyoming ranch gave me
steady work and pay. Less trouble
in old age.

The boots I wear aren't finely polished leather.
I'm an old shoe person, always have been.
Plowing, planting, chasing sheep and cattle
down and up the countryside,
I am of this earth,
feel in my bones I'll return to it soon.

America has entered the war in Europe.
Prices are going up. Everything
is changing. Little is ever in our control.

I thought I was an upright man,
a man of principle, doing my best to provide
for the family. My son Leith, my children,
think me a tyrant, a mean bastard.
I don't know how to set things straight.
Too late, I see Leith was right to leave.

Promises made to ranchers and farmers
won't carry him or any of us without wealth
into the future. I want to tell him
I was wrong, wish his name
could be restored.

But I'm sparse earth.
Something in me keeps me
from saying so.

PREPARING FOR CLASS

Cheyenne, Wyoming, 1918
Leith, age 32, Adah's brother

Some soils are rich with organic matter,
loose enough for water and air to reach in.
Some soils have more sorrow waiting
hidden beneath the surface.

I've lived on Nebraska and Wyoming's arid
earth of sand, gravel, and sedges all my life.
This land has shaped me, is my life.

But I love books too, the things their stories
teach about worlds beyond what I know,
the way books enlarge my life, move me
past the desert places inside, carry me
on their word-rivers into territory rich
with new life.

A teacher, I think about the soil needed
for seeds of thoughts, what the harvest
will bring depending on what I do to prepare
the soil when those seeds are watered.

I sit at a wooden table in a small room, oil lamp
beside me, dimly lighting the space nearby
as I consider what fragile words like liberty
and unity might mean for people
in a dry land with little opportunity.

The War in Europe—Americans
were never going to go there.
It wasn't an American war. But now,
men are dying in trenches, and Wyoming
is the war's supply chain. Horse dealers
and sheepherders profit. It has kept Wyoming
from going under.

(continued)

How do I prepare a lesson about the War
in a foreign land given our own history
of war, challenges we've endured, hopes
we've sheltered, and dreams that have collapsed?

Nearly every Wyoming town
has a One Hundred Percent American Society
chapter, promoting actions like what happened
in Lander where citizens carried the high school's
German textbooks to the town center
and burned them.

People spy on each other, turn in neighbors
they think disloyal Americans.

My whole life I've lived beside Germans.
My family's neighbors are German.
My sister Adah's husband too.

Some people have more tears
waiting inside their skin.

How do I prepare a lesson
to teach the War's hard-gravel facts, turn
through dry soil, bring needed water and air,
plant seeds for a bountiful imagination
of a different story despite, or even because of
the hard-skinned earth we've known?

ADELLA WATCHES CLOUDS WITH JASPER

Chugwater, Wyoming, 1918
Adella, age 61, Adah's mother

It seemed unlike him, but he wanted a cot pulled
from the house and put under the sky.

I held his hands as he lay there dying.
As if children again, we named the shapes in clouds

as they drifted by. Dancing bears, a cherub,
a flying fish, a rabbit. We stayed that way all day,

observing the menagerie, until he grew silent,
fell asleep. I gazed at his hands' long fingers, limp

and lying there so gently after all the work they'd
done for decades, the years he'd spent tending

animals, our family, building a life, only to lay it down.
But perhaps this had been his sweetest day, a day

of complete rest, a long day of not yearning for anything
to be different than it was—simply meandering

amongst imagination's vaporous carousel
coasting above the earth's embrace.

Eyes closed, breath rattling him into a second birth,
he drifted with the mists.

With a slow, near weightless sigh, his last breath
escaped his body, all disappointments and obligations

dissolved into the scape of clouds.
What would happen now, I couldn't fathom,

but I'd never seen his face so soft,
so light.

THE SHIFT

Chugwater, Wyoming, 1918
Adella, age 61, Adah's mother

The wind rose like a river and flooded the land,
exhaled daylight into shadow after Jasper died.

Jamie got out candles. Cedric and Avery lit them.
We sat beside his body listening to his absence

fill the room. As candles burned down, we discussed
what we needed to do. Nothing was normal.

Next day I put on my apron again, went about chores—
fed animals, made soup, did dishes, every few minutes

my actions interrupted by remembering he wasn't
going to call across the yard or walk around the corner

asking for a glass of water, wasn't going to fill
his shoes or put on his hat at the door.

It was spring, but the world never seemed so bare,
so still.

Jasper wasn't the kindest man or tender,
but had grown quieter in the past year, milder.

Avery and I were the only family left at home.
At sixty-two, I took stock of who I was,

what Avery and I could do. No room to dream.
We needed to depend on more than ourselves

to survive. Four months later, the flu arrived.
Schools and libraries closed. Shops allowed

only a few at a time inside. Hospitals filled.
Around me people were dying.

Men had died in battles in countries I'd never seen,
but more were dying here at home than perished

in all those battles. Like breath or thought,
loss unfurled everywhere.

The world had changed. There was no passage back
to the way things used to be. I had to change too.

I always thought his death would bring diminishment.
My life would be reduced.

What I found was the opposite.
I had to widen like the plains, become the sky.

GARDENING

Des Moines, Iowa, 1918
Adah, age 29

I never guessed I'd one day leave Wyoming,
but I like seeing new places, don't mind putting
down new roots even if they'll be shallow
like this crabgrass I pulled up today.

Some people like my brother Leith want
to forget their roots. Makes me wonder
how he'll teach his students when his history
with Father is too painful to remember.
Father's dead now, but thoughts of him
can still sting.

I'm working to make a garden
at Gerard's parents' house here in Des Moines.
I plant and mulch, weed and water, trim back
dead leaves from iris and daffodils, celebrate
the potatoes' arrival, harvest beans and peas.
I care for the garden, and it gives me
bright blooms and fruit hanging from long vines.
So much life!

Still, how many times have I stepped on
a new-sprung bluebell or calendula,
not meaning to,
or when pulling up a dandelion,
broken off a pansy still trying to grow?

When he cut Leith's name from the family Bible,
was it an accident that Father removed my name
from the page too? No one mentioned it,
but I felt the cut.

No matter how we faithfully dedicate ourselves
to care for another. Still, we carry a weight
of ignorance along with us as well.
Still, we step on each other blindly.

Creating a garden requires patience.
Every day I'm bending over a hundred times,
I'm on my knees pulling weeds.

One thing I know for certain,
it takes humility to tend a garden.

Six

LOVE AND WORK
1919–1929

LAUNDRY WOMEN, ADAH'S WORK

Cheyenne, Wyoming, 1919
Adah, age 30

I've sorted, soaked, scrubbed, rinsed, leaned over
washtubs and washboards since childhood.
I know about keeping things clean.

An endless mound of soiled clothes wait
six days a week. We laundry women at Fort Russell
arrive, apron over dress, hair in a bun tucked beneath
caps, to stoop over steamy tubs of sudsy water,
lifting wet jackets, shirts and water-laden sheets.
Carrying water, then heating it, ironing
and mending—no matter the weather,
we wash.

Snow on the ground and freezing water, endless
scrubbing trying to make things right, scrubbing
through broken threads until our hands grow raw
and hearts numb, turn hard as bone.

Like everyone I've known, laundry women
carry stains. We have a reputation
for being opinionated, coarse, argumentative,
and able to be rented for sex.

When people train their eyes to see the stain
in us, the fabric somehow doesn't seem to matter.
How do any of us come clean?

Years go by slumped over steaming water straining,
rinsing through unspoken definitions
of your fabric's shape, how it needs alteration
or repair, when what a woman really wants
is to discover for herself the fabric she's made of,
the garment she wants to wear, what it is
she's fit for beyond what others desire.

Ask me what my job is, and I'll tell you
laundry supervisor. But my real work
is allowing women to provide for themselves,
to make their way in a world that believes
the pleasure taken from a woman's body
is necessary to men's happiness—when women
are the ones who wash their clothes so the men
can keep their pride, clean appearance, and respect.

JAMIE'S QUESTION

Chugwater, Wyoming, 1922
Jamie, age 25, Adah's sister

We're not told the story and will never learn
the whole of it. Only know what I do
because I was in the kitchen when Mother
read the letter. The words stuck in her throat
when she spoke, "Zilda's husband shot
and killed her. Damned filthy fool!"

Mother's hand trembled as she set the letter down.
Turning away, she grabbed a knife and began
to furiously chop an onion. "Hateful hard-headed
witless ass! His jealous rage, and my sister's dead."
She stabbed at an onion with her knife's razor-pointed
edge, tears trickling down her face.

Onion finished, she turned to the nearby potatoes,
cut the eyes out, then struck through each one, knife
hitting the cutting board with a whack
before chucking them into the pot for the fire.

Again, potatoes for dinner.

How many ways can a woman fix and eat
the same food? Over and over, a consistently
recurring fare with minimal variety—boiled, baked
or fried in lard—enough nutrition to keep a body alive,
but holding the barest variation in mealy texture,
that god-awful tasteless flavor.

Rarely does the meal have a delicate taste,
the fullness, or delight one longs for and needs.
I taste the food females are fed, the diet of rage
and rules doled out. Hell, my whole family
is already in torment, why is anyone damned
for what they didn't choose to do?

When the roll is called up yonder,
likely I won't be there.

People say I'm a wild one—I like a drink, a smoke,
and know how to swear. I swear I've no choice
but to marry, must concede to that to survive,
but why would anyone bring a child
into this wicked world?

WHAT SEPTEMBER'S LIGHT SUGGESTED

Cheyenne, Wyoming, 1920
Adah, age 31

September's yellow light ripples the grass
where horses graze. Above the fields, clouds
bloom like puffs of yarrow.

My sister Edra gave birth to her first child,
Frieda, several weeks ago. She's a quiet girl,
Edra says. Peaceful, like her name.

Give birth to anything, and you leave the life
you had. Edra loves working outside with horses.
How will she do that now she has Freida?

Right now, life is as good as I've known it.
But if someday Gerard gets tired of me
and takes off with somebody else,

I don't want to be scrounging for work,
living in some cold, godforsaken shack
trying to scrape money together to eat.

I couldn't bear that
if I had a child to care for too.

How'd I teach a child to stand on her own feet
and have strength enough left to be as kind
as I wish for others to be to me

when I'm still trying to hold myself up?
People say Margot is my "spitting image."
She was a wild teen for Jed and Lenore.

Ran around late at night, smoked and swore.
Trees grow up naturally. Not people.
Raising a child is no small thing.

"One child was hard enough," Lenore explained to me.
"Too abrasive on the heart." She didn't want
to do it again. I showed her what I knew
to help her keep it that way.

Margot doesn't need me to complicate her life
by telling her I'm her mother.
I only birthed Margot. Lenore raised her.
She's the real mother.

History and my body like to send messages
saying it'd be a good idea to have a child
before it's too late.

Gerard would prefer we didn't.

A soothing coolness rustles the fields,
ripples through streets.
Ranchers are planting this season's wheat.

Afternoon's light drenches the room.
I set the dinner table for two.

I'm good with that.

MY MOTHER'S HANDS

Chugwater, Wyoming, 1923
Adella, age 66, Adah's mother

Fingers curled, knuckles swollen with arthritis,
her head encircled by lamplight, I see my mother
bent over her hands, embroidering flowers
on tablecloths, then rubbing at the pain,
though there was little she had to relieve
the aching tenderness that came
from work she did all day
for years
as she milked and mended,
hauled water, and lugged hay.

Despite the hurt, she kept her hands moving,
shaping and reshaping her world, not deterred
by the pain, handing on what she could to me.

When young, I didn't comprehend her aches—
how age alters a woman. Old now, I notice
joints that ache when moved, the hidden places
worn enough for tenderness to emerge.

When Jasper died, the life I lived died too.
Married now to Joel, a blacksmith, I've entered
a different world. Things break, and Joel
remakes and fixes them. Taking damaged saws
and wagon wheels, worn out horseshoes, ruined
tools, he heats the metal from dark carnelian
to opal white, and then strikes the steel over
and over, sparks flying as he reshapes
with his hammer. Form renewed,
he quenches it with water.
Restoration can be brutal.

I'm not a blacksmith but know something
about hammers. I've given birth nine times,
had two children and a husband die, known drought,
hunger and ongoing uncertainty—so many
unanticipated ways things wear down
before they fall apart.

It's true, Joel drinks. Some may say that's a fault,
but I've given him my hand in marriage, worn as it is.
He knows about broken things and tenderness.

Hearts and habits stiff as iron can be melted, renewed
when there's someone who knows how to mend them.

ADAH AND JAMIE'S NEW ROLE

Cheyenne, Wyoming, 1924
Adah, age 35

With plush carpets, telephones, fine leather furniture,
elevators, mahogany finishing work, marble floors,
and private baths, Cheyenne's Plains Hotel
was an elegant establishment attracting wealthy men.

When Gerard finished painting rooms there,
the hotel manager asked him if he knew a woman
who could "'supervise' the girls who entertained
men at the Inn." I could share the work with Jamie
and continue to supervise the women at Fort Russell's
laundry too. So, I agreed, and took on the new role.

Our new work began with two floors of women,
but I had my favorites. Irene had a voice like butter,
a head thick with curls, and loved music.
Sharp-witted Lillian wore rich colors
and donned moods that flickered like fire.
An elusive scent of spiced rose trailed Grace
wherever she went, her eyes pools of dark water,
her wrists a jingle of bangles.

A paradise walled off in a distant time,
the women's dreams reached beyond
those I imagined—to play the piano, own
a clothing store, travel to New York—
their work a means to find a life they wanted
while dealing with daily life and men's desires.

People sell furniture, food, and clothes made
with their own hands, think nothing of selling
their labor, as my father and brothers do—
working twelve hours a day, sometimes more,
their efforts given over to men far wealthier,
while my family labors to put shoes on their feet,
food on the table.

This land is full of wind's blustery force
and tempestuous gales. I've known that wind
all my life.

What the soul is, what is precious and pure,
is difficult to understand in a world that appears
to be flat outside the window, though invisible barriers
rise like mountains when a woman
rides out into the world's wilderness,
trying to work out her salvation.

In Genesis, Tamar used her body and wit
to take charge of her own destiny
and claim her rights.

Jamie and I were helping women do just that.

A PROPER WOMAN

Cheyenne, Wyoming, 1926
Adah, age 37

"Evangelist Aimee Semple McPherson,
who disappeared mysteriously last month
from Santa Monica's Venice Beach
has reappeared," the radio announces.

She drew a crowd larger than President Wilson did
when he visited LA. "I was kidnapped, drugged,
and tortured," she reports, "but escaped
through cutting my bonds on a metal can lid."

Throughout the country, tens of thousands
come to hear her preach. She tells them
they need divine healing and her Savior.
"Help save the heathens abroad and right here,"
she pleads to the listening throngs.
But what I like about her
is that this woman
saved herself.

She's theatrical, likes costumes and props.
Who's to say if her faith healings are real.
But she's a woman men listen to. She cuts
through the handcuffs of limitations, invents
her own possibilities.

Some reporters say her kidnapping story
is a lie. Here in Cheyenne, some say
I, too, am living a lie.
Sometimes I go to church. Wearing hat
and polished shoes, I sit in a pew,
hands folded inside my good gloves,
legs crossed as if a proper woman
though I manage a brothel.
Perhaps I'm one of Aimee's heathens,
but I help women survive.

Respected men in this town own brothels,
believe them vital to business.
People say men must have their wants
fulfilled to be a real and proper man.

My husband Gerard is a respected man
with skill, a member of the painter's union.
When it comes to marriage, though, there's a lot
of unspoken expectations. Who's supposed
to darn the socks and fix dinner, who repair
the stopped-up sink or keep the books?
These are predetermined tasks. Neither of us
has much skill when it comes to other matters.

When Gerard asks me what I want, I've learned
he's telling me instead what he'd prefer I choose.
Marriage is a ride on a settler's Conestoga wagon.
We make a commitment we don't truly understand,
and start out traveling through unfamiliar countryside
over bumpy roads and across swollen rivers, uncertain
where we're headed. We look for a good place to live,
repair a broken wheel or two, drawn on by tradition's
internal compass that tells us what we need to do:
This is the way it is.
Just keep going.

I give loans to neighbors in need, and clothes
to my sister Edra's children.
I don't want to live a lie. As if a Cinderella,
I try to fit into the shoes of a good woman and wife.

Most women live the life they're given.
I hang a crucifix on the wall, say prayers,
and hope to be counted as "good."

How do I love my husband and still
cut free from rules I never made
but am meant to follow?

Aimee quotes her Jesus, "Come unto me
all you who labor and are heavy laden."   (continued)

What I want to learn is how I can have faith enough
to be healed from infirm ideas that tell me
I am what others say—that my roles and flaws
are who I am.
Salvation doesn't always wear a hat, gloves,
and polished shoes.
Sometimes it looks like a woman standing beside
a woman with a bruised and broken heart in a brothel,
cross strung around her neck, the suffering
she's endured for want of love
who manages, still, to carry herself
with grace.

We need a metal lid stronger than Aimee's
to save ourselves.

A WOMAN WITH SASS

Cheyenne, Wyoming, 1927
Frank, age 34, Adah's brother-in-law, Jamie's husband

Jamie puts on her trousers every morning, ready
for duties at the laundry, then later, work at the hotel
with Adah. Who'd guess a woman in overalls
manages prostitutes? Jamie's sharp—
knows a few things. No question,
she's able to take charge.

Jamie meets a lot of men, arranges connections
for them. I don't like her around those high-class
men coming to the hotel, making business deals,
anticipating a woman at an agreement's end.
It could be tempting to be coaxed into
an arrangement on the side.

A woman in overalls won't appeal to most.
Underneath those overalls
is a woman with muscles.

A horse trainer, I like a good ride
and Jamie knows how. She can lasso a steer,
cuss with the best. She's got nerve.

I don't like the way Gerard won that piece
of turquoise from me in a card game,
or the way he goes to the hotel every day,
supposedly to see Adah, but spends time
with Jamie too, going over accounts.

True, they're both good with numbers.
Jamie brings home money we need, but I
hate how she spends time with Gerard,
works too late.

(continued)

I drink beers at the bar, wait for her to get home.
When she arrives, she knows what I want.
But all I get is her anger for "wasting
her good money" with a few drinks.
She pushes me away.

"I'm not a damn horse," she shouts.
"You can't control me."

Over and over, the same story.
I slam the door, go find a woman
who'll give me what I want.

THE PANTS I WEAR

Cheyenne, Wyoming, 1927
Jamie, age 30, Adah's sister

I was wrenching knotted weeds from the ground
outside the house when I realized
I had to divorce Frank.

He's a tangled snarl of drink, jealousy, and anger
that clutches at me like crabgrass, a weed
that chokes my life with alcohol,
shouts, and fear.

A year and half of that is enough to know
the weeds in his head won't stop growing
because I want them to.

If he suspects I've spoken with a man,
Adah's husband Gerard included, he goes crazy,
accuses me of two-timing when he's the one
who carries on with other women
while telling me to stay at home.

A horse trainer, Frank is used to being in control.
He can read a horses' behavior, predict
when they'll bite, kick, or toss a rider,
but with me he's the horse who runs wild.

I'm not a tame woman,
I admit.
But I expect respect.

I'll have to prove to the courts
Frank's an adulterer, lay everything in the open.
I've got evidence.

(continued)

I did it before when I divorced Harold.
I'll do it again.
Twice divorced when divorce is disgraced—
I'm already branded, what's another?

I have a job. Two, in fact.
One at the laundry, one helping Adah
manage the brothel, though the pay
still isn't much.

Women wearing pants
aren't seen in a good light.
I reject that.

Starting today
I'm putting on my rebel pants.

THE GEOMETRY OF LOVE

Cheyenne, Wyoming, 1927
Cedric, age 28, Adah's brother

Della was born in Wisconsin. Her history isn't mine,
but unexpected encounters can change a life.

Meeting Della where I work at the bank was
one of those surprises—her kind, steady eyes,

laughter's lilt, sure step. I'm only twenty-eight,
but I've observed many ways people are divided

over beliefs, and money. The rich work to multiply
their assets, while to get by, many others

must subtract from theirs. A bookkeeper,
I record numbers, notice patterns and figure out

relationships, but marriage isn't a mathematical
formula to follow to find an answer to a problem.

I can't answer where the future will carry us,
but my life doesn't have to be like my parents'.

I'm choosing Della because one and one
is much more than two every time I've imagined

adding our lives together. We're more than separate
family lines intersecting for practical purposes,

greater than the measure of difference between
the angles of worlds we come from. I choose Della

because of her story's differences.
Today, we promised ourselves to each other

in marriage. I looked into Della's trusting face
as she stood before me in her simple blue dress,   *(continued)*

our lives stretched infinitely wide,
everything we are meeting at the heart's

center point. I placed the ring on her finger.
We said, "I do," then

stepped through the door into a wheatfield,
gold beyond calculation.

CELEBRATING THE ORDINARY

Beaver Creek, Weston, Wyoming, 1929
Lenore, age 46, Adah's sister

There are a thousand sweetnesses in this world
unknown to me, but one I do know is chocolate.

Collecting coins from eggs I sell, every now and then,
I buy sweets. Selecting one chocolate a day, I savor it,
hold it in my mouth until it melts completely,
and I've dissolved with it the weary parts of my day.

When the box is finished, I put it on a shelf
in the back room. Some I cover with bright ribbon
and delicious fabric, others with fancy paper
designed with roses or a landscape with trees,
mountains, and lake.

Edra sometimes comes by with her kids.
I bring them to the shelf. "You may pick
any box you want," I say.
Some boxes are plain, some fancy. "Only one
contains a chocolate I've put inside."

Hovering over the boxes, carefully examining
them—soft satin fabric over a heart-shaped
form or simple rectangular ones with no frills,
the children choose. Box in hand they raise the lid,
hoping for a sweet.

After Jed forced himself on Adah years ago now,
I wanted to believe he still contained the sweetness
I saw in him when first we met.
Love honors boundaries,
offers respect.
I didn't trust that he did.

(continued)

I worked all day, fed Margot and the chickens,
invented recipes, did chores. At night
I lay awake and alone, picturing my heart
stretch over the bleak fields to the far horizon
where the sun rose in yellow light.
Had to make myself grow larger
than the scrunched down hole
I felt I'd been shoved into.
Had to be bigger for Margot.
She was our child now.

Margot's childhood tantrums, then later
her teenage willfulness opened Jed's eyes:
Relationship requires patience,
understanding, and respect.

We've had our difficulties and failures
but focus now on the good we find.

Some evenings Jed and I sit on our steps,
watch clouds turn caramel-gold then plum
before sinking into evening's dark chocolate.
It an ordinary thing, sitting together,
but dear.

Chocolate makes a long journey to reach
these plains. To discover a sweet inside
a small, unadorned box in late afternoon
when expecting something better
out of the one with ribbons or lace,
that is a happiness to savor
when everything else
seems to have dissolved.

Seven

Turnings
1930–1935

PLANING WOOD

Cheyenne, Wyoming, 1930
Gerard, age 45, Adah's husband

Wood curls fall to the floor. I'm planing a board
for a cabinet, working the wood's surface
to make sure the uneven places turn smooth,
remembering how thirteen years ago
I registered for the draft though I didn't need to.
Adah agreed, it seemed like a smart idea.
Best to avoid planing against the grain.
A good carpenter knows to check his work
so that his boards sit flush
against adjacent wood.

My parents were born in France
but are from German descent. Their heritage
scared people during the War.

Still does.

An American born in Iowa, I'm many things:
a husband, son, brother, a neighbor, and friend,
but it's harder to get work when people believe
your surname could mean you're an enemy or spy.

I live on a plain, but invisible mountains
rise everywhere.

Luckily, Adah has work at the base and the hotel,
brings in enough to keep us going, as well as to give
loans to some who've come against hard times.

I place a straight edge against the wood's surface,
then turn the board to make sure
there's no gaps with a high spot,

plane a bit more.

FIGHT

Cheyenne, Wyoming, 1930
Adah, age 41

As every washerwoman knows, grass stains,
wine, ink and iron are difficult to remove.
Despite a woman's work to boil, scrub,
wring, and rinse, soiled clothes might require
a treatment of chloride of lime, sorrel salt drops,
turpentine, or a few days soaking
in a buttermilk bath to bring them clean.

Yesterday Jamie came late to work at the hotel,
clothes still wet and unkempt from leaning over
steaming pots at the laundry all day.
"Rooms need to be straightened, beds made,"
I complained. The hotel boss expected
perfection. I marked her entry time
and closed the book. "People are waiting."

A piercing poker, her eyes bored into me,
ready to turn boiling water into frigid ice.
Her mouth twisted tight then sprung on me
like a metal trap. "You self-centered goat!
For you there's nothing but rules, rules,
rules, as if I'm some small worm
who wants nothing more than to dig
into your tidy, laced up life!"

Jamie knew we had to follow rules
if we wanted this work. I could argue,
tell her how the hotel boss jumped on me
about our hours in the books.
We needed to keep a good reputation.

"I'm not a senseless stone, Adah.
Our whole family knows about rules.

(continued)

Cedric makes sure those bigwigs at banks
follow them so people don't lose their shirts.
Leith's class of forty students need rules
so words can be heard."

Her voice rose into a train's rumbled roar,
shook the space between us, echoed
through the hollow spaces inside me.

"Good God, Adah, I know about rules.
You, me, Lenore, Mama, all of us—all we heard
from day one with Father was how we had to
follow rules. Did you think to ask
what happened to me, why I'm still
wearing wet clothes, my hair full of muck?"

The floor creaked beneath my foot.
My mind went blank.
Stock-still, I waited for the blasts yet to come.
What was going on beneath her words
I didn't know, but realized to her
I'd become our father.

"You, with your perfect hair bun, fine fabrics,
lace collars. Me in my overalls.
I'm a grubby low-down laborer, Adah.
You know that.
I worked at the Cambria mines, for God's sake.
Men stooped inside that coal mine's dark hell hole,
wheezing, coughing their living daylights out.
They followed every rule. Where'd it get them?
There's more important things than rules, Adah."

We stood there in the room's broken light
staring at each other. Walls
quiet now as gravestones.

Tentatively, I fumbled for her hand,
hoped she wouldn't push me away
as if some soiled rag.

THOUGHTS WHILE WALKING

Cheyenne, Wyoming, 1931
Cedric, age 32, Adah's brother

The "Star Spangled Banner," adopted as the national
anthem this year, was sung today at Cheyenne's
Frontier Days rodeo. I listened, then watched
men wrestle steer and ride bucking bulls.

Rodeos aren't my favorite pastime, but it's
a big event in Cheyenne and times are tough,
so I went for a few hours.
Afterwards, I walked beside Crow Creek.

A bank examiner now who makes sure banks
follow rules, I wanted the creek's quiet murmur
to help me think about why so many banks
are going under, wanted to consider what it means
to be a citizen, to belong to a country,
a place.

People like my father came to these plains
with hope of owning land, the freedom
to create a life without the wealthy
thwarting their dreams.

Trains brought supplies—clothes, staples,
and tools people depended on for survival.

I look across these yellow fields beside me
and recall how bison once filled this land.
Indians relied on them for food, clothes,
and shoes—used their hides for shelter.

But bison disrupted train lines.
Rail companies hired men to hunt them.
Hunting parties of hundreds
shot the animals from train roofs and windows,
killed, and left them. *(continued)*

Thirty million buffalo dead in two decades.
No way for tribes to sustain their lives
without them—
and the West opened.

Sweeping landscape, wide skies, cowboys,
rodeos—these identify the West,
but the War, coal and oil mining—these
kept Wyoming going.

The War drove prices high.
Without enough workers, farmers turned
to tractors, went into debt to buy them.

Oil boomed. But drought caused farmers
to struggle. Prices fell.
Then the choking dirt storms came,
and banks collapsed.

I should've seen it coming.
Wealth isn't disconnected from the land,
promises we make,
or how we treat each other.

Laws benefit most
the ranchers with the largest herds,
farmers with the greatest means.

But things can change.
Like the trail I'm walking now, a path
can turn narrow, rocks appear, water
cover the way through.
Mud.

Father's dead now.
Rhoda and Shara died years ago,
but there are losses I don't think about—
    lives lost to mine explosions,
    lungs scarred with coal soot,
    Indians pressed into reservations.
There's a sting inside nearly everything.

Like neighbors whose savings, land,
and way of life vanished, I don't notice
everything I see.

Beyond ignorance, loss, fear, and greed,
a stillness continues to hold and bear us—
the land beneath, a great body of quiet
felt with feet.

I keep walking.

WHAT HAPPENED TO FRANK

Cheyenne, Wyoming, 1931
Gerard, age 46, Adah's husband

It hadn't rained in ages. A great cloud of soil
lifted from the earth and rode high into the sky.

I shifted my work from painting
after the soil-blizzard arrived,
am a cabinet maker now.

I'd put the drill, saw, and c-clamps away,
and counted the money from the cabinets
I made for the Horticultural Field Station
when someone banged on the door.

I didn't want to take chances.
Robbed before, I took the gun from my desk,
put it in my pocket beside the turquoise
I won from Frank in a card game, keep there
for good fortune, and went to answer
the noise outside.

It was Frank.
His frame filled the space, face serious.
"Have a matter to settle," he said, nervous.

His breath said he'd been drinking, a reason
Jamie divorced him three years before.
Cautiously, I let him in.

As if the blizzard of suspended dirt outside
had entered, the air turned suddenly tight.

He stared at the wood shavings on the floor.
"My horse training business has gone under.
Can't make a living."
I felt the weight in his voice.

"Between drought, the Depression, divorce—"
his voice trailed off.
It wasn't an easy conversation.
I thought he might want a loan.

He stepped directly in front of me, eyes intense.
"You spent time with Jamie in one of those rooms
Adah and her rent by the hour." His voice
erupted in a whip snap. Spit sprayed my face.
I backed away, didn't want to rile him further.

"I didn't," I told him.

Frank lunged forward, mouth distorted,
body shaking, "Damn you!" he shouted,
arms slicing the air. "You're why Jamie left me!
I got nothing! Money Jamie and Adah collect
from the women at the Plains Hotel could've been
mine. You cheated on me with Jamie,
cheated me out of money."

His shoulders shuddered.
I tried to speak, but he bellowed on.
"You ruined me!" He lunged forward,
shoved me down.

"You're a damn Kaiser-loving lowlife liar."
His boot exploded against my back.

"You Catholics lie when you call yourself Christian.
Shit, what kind of Christian allows his wife
to run a brothel?
You're not goin' home to nobody
no more. You're going to hell."

He struck his boot against my skull.
My head spun.
I'm not a strong man.
Frank was and he knew it.
Blood throbbed in my ear,
dripped down my face.   (continued)

No reasoning with a drunk deluded with anger,
poisoned with prejudice.

I curled forward to protect myself, felt
for the turquoise stone in my pocket, twisted
'till I got my hand on the gun, then turned
to point and fire, and kept firing,
one sharp burst after another, not knowing
if any shot
would be enough to stop him.

Then, there he was
lying on the floor in his rumpled, thread-bare coat.

Dead.

No going back to rethink
how things might've gone differently,
the words I could've said
if I'd found the thoughts.

Self-defense the judge ruled.

Is justice as simple as one man's wrong
allows a different man to be right?
I was declared innocent
but don't feel right.
I killed a man.

Forgiving myself is another matter.
When I see Jamie, my thoughts return
to Frank lying on the floor,
room thick with the scent of sulfur.
Death can arrive in a moment, but the memory
doesn't die.

Frank imagined the story he wanted to be right,
but the cause of his problems was bigger,
more complex. What if we can't bear
the difficulties we're given?

Frank's blunt accusations and loss stir
the heap of other flaws and past mistakes
I've never escaped.
They all pound against me
with heavy boots.

Forgiveness requires change.
Painting and new cabinets can give a fresh look
to a room. Sometimes these aren't enough.
The room itself needs alteration,
a different shape,
walls torn down, a new design.

I'm a painter, a cabinet maker.
I don't know how to move walls.

Neither did Frank.

THE CHRISTMAS MOTHER

Custer, South Dakota, 1932
Edra, age 37, Adah's sister

My daughter Freida begged me to go to the gathering.
        She loves the friendship and songs, but I'm not
sure about religion. I didn't give in because of her
prodding. I like going places, so August and I
        piled the family into the wagon.

It was a rare, dangerous thing, and I won't forget it:
        a Christmas tree lit with candles. Carefully,
we clipped candleholders to the tree that held
tapers, the counterweights dangling below
the branches.

Then, one by one lit the candles. Where before
the room was filled with excited chatter, now
an intense quiet
        settled a softness over the house.

Water bucket ready, everyone stared intently
        at the flame-lit tree, hoping nothing
would catch fire.

No one moved.

        For a few moments, lost in the flickering light
            and pine scent as if in dream, silence
absorbed us.

Someone sang "Silent night, holy night..."
Others joined. There I stood in my work boots,
        knit cap and bib overalls, the walls around us
            tired and worn, though Freida's eyes
glowed as if candle fire.

I'm not a soft woman. I've wrung chicken's necks,
        chased pigs with a shotgun, butchered them
        for their meat.
Don't know if I believe in virgin births.
Unmarried women I know who've given birth

aren't respected. Yet there we were singing
        to this mother's honor. That was miracle.
                The singing stopped. People turned
to talk. We blew out the candles, and the room

returned to normal. We left to ride home
through December's sharp cold under a star-spilled sky,
        children huddled in the wagon's hay.

The memory of the candles' brief light
        in the night-dark room a whisper
faint as smoke from a far fire.

AVERY'S INSIGHT

Chugwater, Wyoming, 1933
Avery, age 40, Adah's brother

Though I can dance, I could never make an engine
like my brother Leith, am not good at math like Cedric.
I look in the mirror and notice how small my eyes are.

It's been nine years since Mr. Hubble announced he found
other galaxies. Ours isn't the only one. But worlds
always have spun beyond what I can make sense of.

Whirling stardust, giant holes in the sky, spacious gaps
between starlight. Worlds lie hidden inside what's seen.
The stars on Orion's belt could be galaxies.

I know how to turn a plow to till. Focusing on one row
at a time is the way I move through a pasture, as well as
how I make it through the world. Sometimes when I'm

preparing a field in the morning beneath the bowl
of sky, plow moving rhythmically through the soil,
the world turns into a kind of music, and I sense

everything is dancing to a melody just beyond
what I can hear. I look at the horizon and sense
I'm a pebble in a field that can be turned by a plow.

Everything is larger than anyone will ever understand.

LEITH'S NEW OPPORTUNITY

Cheyenne, Wyoming, 1934
Leith, age 48, Adah's brother

Winter can be cruel. Sixty-six below zero
in Yellowstone last year. Glad I don't live there.
Minus nine in Cheyenne is cold enough.

Growing up, Mother compared the cold
I complained about to the winter of '86,
just before I was born. The Great Die-Up.
Fierce storms for months in a row. Heavy snows,
cold so deep cattle had no fodder, froze
while standing-up—hundreds of thousands died.
The notion of nature's limitless abundance
finished off, cattle drives across open range
ended.

Trains made life on the plains possible,
changed the land.
The world is changing.
Who can make a living as a farmer
or rancher now, and who as a teacher?
I left teaching. As Father predicted,
I couldn't support a family on the salary.

Hoover believed in big projects, promoted
building bridges, tunnels, freeways,
and the dam at the Arizona-Nevada border
when president. FDR's New Deal now funds them.

With new opportunities as an engineer, I helped plan
service roads, water and sewer systems
for the Civilian Conservation Corps.
Jobs are scarce, but I've assisted developing
designs for a museum at Guernsey Park, a stone castle,
and a boat dock the CCC men are now building.

(continued)

Land reclamation projects, the Post Theater
at Fort Warren—work I do improves lives,
now as well as in the future
with pay allowing me not to worry.

First, the 1918 pandemic at the century's start
filled hospital beds and obituaries.

Then, thousands upon thousands of jackrabbits
descended across the land, desperate for food,
eating grass and crops down to their roots.

Later, hordes of frantic locusts gorged on corn
and razed fields. Swarms spread miles wide,
billions of undulating wings beating, clicking.
Locust-waves broke across the earth.
As if alive, the land convulsed,
crackled. Throbbed.

Static electricity arced the sky, blue flame
jumping, snapping across barbed wire fences.
A whirlpool of purple-black dust
two miles high, twice the amount of earth
removed when Panama's Canal was dug
darkened the sky, choked the breath,
inflamed the lungs.

Many left the life they wanted here
but could no longer have,
escaping to California.

Even as some of my neighbors went hungry,
the government gave struggling farmers
money to not raise cattle, pigs, and wheat
while agents shot cattle and pigs
by the tens of thousands.

The path through loss isn't linear.
A bitter weight to behold,
we're manifesting our destiny.
I was a teacher,
but now everything teaches me.

We save our money to pay the rent.
No thought of new shoes.
A minimum wage was recently created,

still, many like those in my family, subsist
on the margins their entire lives
while others are given benefits,
opportunity.

What is our sacred duty now?
So much we don't comprehend
about our destiny.
Why is it sorrow persists?

For some dilemmas there's no clear resolution,
just the need to endure the gaps, live
with the questions.

Together we share the world, and the world
is difficult.

REMEMBERING ADELLA

Beaver Creek, Weston, Wyoming, 1935
Lenore, age 52, Adah's sister

We are people of the grasslands.
Except for being six feet tall, my mother
was ordinary as grama grass, buffalo grass—

low to the ground and rarely noticed.
Without grass, soil flies loose, wind carries away
what sustains life.

Like the grass here in Wyoming, bowed by wind,
my mother rooted her life on the plains,
her straight back inclining to its needs.

Every action a prayer of submission to necessary work:
my mother bent over a stove stirring a pot, bent over
newborn sisters and brothers, bent over a pail,

milking sheep; her tall, aproned frame pacing slowly
between sheets as she hung them on a line to dry.
Her body present, then disappearing

between the sheets' stretched lengths, light
breathed through sun's long curve into cloth's
warp and weft, fabric swelling and flapping in wind's

funnel. Her body visible, going about work, then
invisible. The strength it took to bend and lift
their wet weight.

Now I bend over her on her deathbed,
on this day full of wind, as she lies between
sheets she washed so often.

I see her body's weft giving itself breath by breath
to the light, evaporating from her, lifting its weight.
Her efforts, like the effort of ten thousand strands

of ordinary grass—all us ordinary, commonplace people,
and the labor we give ourselves to,
that holds together the soil of life.

I see what you did, Mother. I remember.

MATTERS OF CHOICE, ADAH'S NEW WORLD

Cheyenne, Wyoming, 1935
Adah, age 46

Say it was self-defense. Say Frank was a deluded,
angry, and self-centered man. Say he should've
accepted things as they were, and all would be well.

Say it took five bullets because Gerard was a bad shot
and afraid. Say Gerard was declared innocent
because Frank intruded on our property
and threatened Gerard, but the griefs in the world
felt larger after Gerard killed Frank.

We sent Jamie a telegram—would she come
to the funeral? "No," she said.
"Too much misery already from that wretched prune.
Don't want to revisit that foul hellhole
or torture myself with more."

Gerard grew sick. We took to ambling along
Crow Creek to watch heron along the banks
feed on fish, and observe warblers make their nests,
a world that carried us beyond worries
about the way we wanted things to be
but weren't.

Cutting costs and struggling to make ends meet,
the depression in Wyoming started a decade
before the New York stock market crashed.

Money I'd received from women at the Plains Hotel
I loaned to people about to lose their property—
holding their deeds as collateral while waiting
for their lives to recover.

When Gerard grew too ill to walk,
I sometimes walked with Ivan, a man I met
where I worked at the laundry.

"You're making an ass of yourself again," Jamie said.
Married women didn't go on walks with men.

I knew it wasn't acceptable. But I wanted Ivan
as a friend. He wasn't like other men.
He saw the world as I never had.

"The world is held together by light," he told me
as we watched birds slip through a sunset sky.

I wasn't sure what he meant, but I felt light
when walking with him, the way I did when a child
wandering through grassy fields, the world around me
opening into layer upon layer of wind-touched fields
rising into summits of billowed cloud.

Then Gerard died
and everything pivoted.

Gerard's connection to the community,
his steady income and ongoing presence—
I used to say he worked too much, but he
was the stable ground that held my world.
Now that ground had collapsed,
not for others, but for me.

The world I knew disappeared,
and it wasn't my choice.

Farmers and ranchers, the elderly, women
without partners, those who live on reservations—
they've been clinging to the cliff-side of life
for years, trying to keep from falling off.

How did my father, my mother, my sisters—
how do any of us endure past the weighted
collapse of one world after another?

Say the whole world was crawling through
a desert of depression. But also say,
for some there are far fewer choices
of how to survive.

Eight

Dust
1936–1944

THE HEART OF SOMEWHERE

Beaver Creek, Weston, Wyoming, 1936
Jed, age 73, Adah's brother-in-law
Lenore, age 53, Adah's sister
Margot, age 28, Adah's daughter

    I.   Jed

Margot was a mule-headed girl with a bad mouth
and rebellious. She snuck around, broke rules.
I tried to smooth the rough spots between us,
but bumbled about trying to be a father to a girl
who didn't want to become the pearl
Lenore and Adah named her for.

    II.   Margot

I broke rules, though Dad tried to smooth
the rough spots. All those qualities they named me for:
purity, peace, perfection—I wasn't interested in that.
I wanted to be the wind kicking up a bit of dirt.

    III.   Lenore

A pearl's peace and purity, Margot was named for these.
I tried to teach her to cook, sew, and take charge
of a house, but she preferred to whirl like wind-stirred
grit. Love is a dust devil. You spin, but don't know
how things will turn out.

    IV.   Margot

Yes, I was a gutsy, rebellious girl who liked to swear.
Then I became a teacher, and had to enforce rules,
coil tight my mind's restless squalls into a smooth-
surfaced pearl of expectations.

Students think me cold, stale, uncaring, but I swear
I'll someday move beyond roles and expectations, cross
the world beyond the clouds of my parent's restless
dreams, journey past places I know or can name.

Beyond the flatland of rules and probability, I spin
my obstinate hope to travel: my heart's lusty pearl
whirling into the windy hopes of somewhere.

MISTAKE

Cheyenne, Wyoming, 1936
Adah, age 47

The clouds hung low to the ground, heavy, ready
to break loose in storm when Raymond
stepped through the door with his perfect buttons
and shining belt buckle, back straight,
chin pointed, head held high.

My workday at the laundry was nearly finished.
I handed him his newly pressed clothes
and he inspected them with approval.

I thought I wanted a trim, firm man,
who appreciated order, knew how
to take charge, a stable man
with steady work.

The world is full of disasters—
people lose their homes, their health,
the ones they love. I'd lost Gerard
long before I expected.
What I couldn't bear after Gerard's death
was the stillness in the house, the dust motes
hanging in the air's static light.

I knew the prejudice against single women,
and had my own questions about where
my life would go if I remained alone.

I wanted better than that.

A coal or oil field worker smelling of mineral,
sediment under the fingernails that wouldn't
wash out, a farmer, railroad man, or cattle rancher—
those men weren't for me.

A clean-cut military man, Raymond seemed
a better option. He knew I was a laundry supervisor,
and what that suggested, said he wanted a woman
with experience.

After we'd married, though, he wanted someone else.

"Your hair's a mess," he'd bluntly pronounce.
"Don't wear that," he'd bark, or curtly state
mid-conversation, "Stop talking!"
then later ask why I never laughed.

Upon entering the house, he'd run his finger
along the door frame and tabletop to see
how well I'd dusted. He followed me to work,
concerned I'd talk with someone
he didn't approve of.

What I don't want to see is how,
like Raymond, I look at others and criticize
their clothes, how they should be cleaner
or their house better kept, how I fault those
whose voices are weak or shrill—
how easily I find shame in others
when daily I see the hundred ways
I'll never be enough.

When Raymond started sleeping around,
I quit cooking and ironing.
I wasn't going to play that role.

I wanted the words to fling in Raymond's face,
curses to cut through his self-perfection,
and petty rules, his delusion
of control.

Instead, I ripped the buttons from his shirts,
drug his jacket through the mud,
slammed the door on the empty house,
went to the courthouse,
and filed for divorce.

DUST

Cheyenne, Wyoming, 1936
Adah, age 47

The light from the lobby's silk shades
veiled the room in a pallid yellow.
A man with a dark jewel decorating
his index finger played last year's tunes
on the grand piano. From the dining room,
drifted the scent of grilled steak.

The hotel manager entered the room
with a stiff smile. Jamie placed our keys
in his outstretched hand. I gave him the ledger.
"Good," he said. "I wish you well,"
then sniffed as we turned to leave.

Our work at the hotel was done.
No word given as to why.
Reasons aren't always reasonable
when someone tells you
you're no longer needed.

I'd learned to wear fashionable clothes
and how to style my hair to please people—
big ranchers, businessmen, bankers,
lawyers, real estate barons—but a glance
just now in the mirror's reflection
on the nearby wall told me
I didn't really fit their worlds.
Didn't want to anymore either.

With the money from my work at the brothel
I bought shoes for my sister Edra's boys
when they had none. When grasshoppers
devoured farmers' crops, I carried the loans
on property for hard-up families. I paid
people's doctor bills, donated to schools,

gave women who worked for me gifts.
I'd brought some good to this city.

A defense for why Jamie and I should
be able to continue working at the hotel
never escaped my mouth. Words
wouldn't change this manager's mind.
I'd never learn the real story. Knew him
well enough for that.

Some things fall apart softly as lint.

Golden as things were for a time,
that life is over.

It was a Sunday morning. The brothel
was closed. The hotel didn't want
to keep anybody from church.

The manager opened the door to the street.
The hotel hallway's frosty scent
blew into a burn of Autumn wind.

Jamie and I wandered down the street.
Droughts and grasshopper infestations,
Gerard's death, our divorces—
we'd been through it all and were still moving.

A short month ago the second World War started.
The grief of our loss was but a strand of dry grass
in the world's wind-tossed weather.

Where we'd end up next, we weren't certain
but we knew we'd be in it together.

AFTER DANCING

Cheyenne, Wyoming, 1937
Adah, age 48

I pull sheets from the mangler's rollers,
hang them to dry in the spring-bright air.
After divorcing Raymond and losing my work
at Cheyenne's hotel, I felt washed out,
wanted a new start.

A movie with a satisfying ending after
lifting wet clothing all day sounded right.
Shall We Dance with Astaire and Rogers
seemed the perfect escape.

I arrived at the theater with women from work, but
when Litton walked down the theater aisle and saw
the empty seat beside me, he chose to sit there.
We'd never met before, but turned to tell each other
what we thought characters would do, and laughed
at the same scenes the whole film through.

When the film finished, we stepped into the street.
I was thinking of the scene where Petrov
tells Linda they'll be going their separate ways
after she'd asked him to marry her
when Litton started singing "They Can't
Take That Away From Me," then began dancing
right there in the street, his feet light as Petrov's.
Litton's a bit crazy, I thought.
But he made me laugh.

Movie romance is a fantasy.
I'm a practical woman.
Living with someone years into the future
requires a lot more than enjoying the ease
of someone's body next to mine when dancing.

I listened to my body anyway.
I wanted him.

Standing here now in the mud beneath the clothesline,
I remember how marriage to Raymond
pressed me down, wrung me through.
Hung me to dry.
That's over.

I'm seven years older than Litton.
He survived WWI. That's sure to have added
years on to his life that equals out our age.

Wind blows through my hair, across my skin,
tosses the sheets to the sapphire sky.
I lift my eyes, let the air's endless openness
fill me.

I'm older now but am not done yet.
Next week Litton and I marry.

Unlike the young woman he was engaged to,
I'm not going to be getting pregnant,
and I like the possibility of movement
that marrying a military man brings.

I never imagined I'd find someone to marry
under lights dim as a movie theater's
where the only illumination
is on a flickering screen.

Like Astaire, Litton's ears are a little large,
but his body is lean and limber. He moves
with natural comfort, dances with polished care,
same as the shine on his shoes. His feet
glide across the earth as if to say
despite the ugliness a body may have
known during war, beauty
is still possible.

(continued)

The sheets on the line lift in the air's arms,
turn, flutter. My arms' strength put them there.
Though pinned, they dance.

Cheyenne's history is wild.
Maybe it's crazy to marry a man
I met a few months ago. I'm sure
my sister Jamie would tell me that.
But I want what life with Litton might bring.
I don't want to be alone.

I can't dance like Ginger Rogers, feet
stepping smoothly across every floor,
tapping in perfect rhythm, turning
at just the right time.

God knows I've tripped many times.
But like Roger's character Linda Keene
who asked Petrov to marry her, I'm ready
to take risks to get what I want.

JAMIE CONSIDERS ADAH'S DECISION

Cheyenne, Wyoming, 1937
Jamie, age 40, Adah's sister

Was it panic, fear of being alone
after twenty-seven years of marriage
that made Adah do it?
Adah could've lived on her own
after Gerard's death. She has his pension,
knew how to make her way, but it was as if
there was a tear in her life she wanted to
stitch up as quickly as possible.

A few short months later she married.
Not Ivan, but Raymond, a browbeating bully,
mean and demeaning like our father.
Too long living with uncertainty growing up,
and she thought she wanted someone with authority.

Adah's strong, feisty, but she's not like me.
Before my first marriage, I washed clothes,
cooked and waited on tables for the single men
at the Cambria mines. Collapsed tunnels, explosions
from underground rooms filled with gas—
mining was dangerous. For some the danger
brought a sense of strength.
You had to be tough.
Lose focus and you could die.

Adah would never do it, but I
started wearing pants at the mines.
It gave me less trouble with bad eggs
like Raymond.

The best paying women's work
is the work women do selling their favors.
That wasn't a life Adah wanted. Besides,
she wasn't young anymore.

(continued)

Marrying a man gives a woman less worry
about money. Raymond had more income
than Ivan, but he'd never be a man
to go on walks with.

Neither was he honorable.

Four months after marriage, she divorced him.
It's not a common choice, but brave,
and right.

I can't guess the inducements Adah used,
but after her divorce, she persuaded Litton,
another military man, to leave his girlfriend
and marry her instead.

How do we untangle what we want
from what we've been told and shown
are the only possibilities?

Like Adah, I'm married to a man
who smokes though I despise the smell
now that I don't smoke.

It takes time to learn who we are,
what we need.

The only assurance of security or respect
Adah knew was to marry a man.
Adah was convinced Litton
would give her that.

PERSPECTIVE

Cheyenne, Wyoming, 1940
Leith, age 54, Adah's brother

The story we're told is not necessarily the story
that's true. I don't know the story anyone
will tell of me in the future, but the story
someone tells of any of us is only partly true.

When my oldest sister Shara died, someone
wrote the cause in the records as typhoid fever,
though the family knew it was a failed abortion.

Father found out Adah got pregnant
and called her careless, but was she
the one to blame?

Mother was a teacher before she married.
People thought it natural she wasn't allowed
to teach once she married, never asked
if she would've liked to extend that portion
of her tale, how it might have helped
our family make ends meet.

The boy I adopted when he was a baby
turned to forging money when he got older
and landed in prison, a story that might
be interpreted as my being too lenient with him
when he was a child.

Jamie once said women made the best lovers,
though three times she married a man,
a story we've never heard the whole of.

We learn a fact, interact with a person a time
or two, and create a story.

(continued)

One story is Father thought I was worthless
when I questioned his authority, his rules,
what he knew and didn't.

"How dare you!" he raged, "when I'm working
all day, tilling land that's mostly clay."

My brothers and sisters fell mute, Father's shouts
pushing them against the room's edges.

"I'm fighting off grasshoppers, pulling potato bugs
from vines so we can have something to eat, hauling
hay, chopping ice so cows can drink in winter,
and you complain about rules, about not wanting
to work on a ranch? Damn you, you worthless boy!"

He found a knife and the family Bible, frantically
flipped to the page where births were recorded,
and in a rage cut me from it, certain the story
he created of how I saw him was the totality
of who I was, though it was a constellation of ideas
he'd formed from stories he'd long held
and told himself about the way things had to be.

But I was looking at the empty spaces inside
his arrangement of information—how he
was caught in the story of a dream
that wasn't going to come right.

The Homestead Act said he could have
160 prairie acres if he could live on
and cultivate it for five years. Railroads
corroborated the government's stories,
described the prairie as a garden spot and fertile.

Speeches and pamphlets proclaimed, "rain
follows the plow," though maps previously
called the area the Great American Desert.

160 acres of irrigated land is too large
for a single family to farm. Our land
wasn't irrigated. We needed more like
2,500 acres for our ranch to succeed.

We left Nebraska, moved to Wyoming near
the Swan Company's headquarters in Chugwater,
but life wasn't going to be much better.

We live by our stories.
I'm one to question stories I was told.
Can't help it.

Constellations have immense gaps.
Ask two people about an event that's occurred,
and you'll get different versions and details.
Father wanted to accept the story he was told,
didn't want to believe his concerted effort
was not going to bring him the world
he wanted to be true.

When Father finished cutting my name
from the Bible, he held up the page.
My birth removed, and on the opposite side
of the page, my death eliminated too.

"Who are you?" I asked, trembling.
Do you see better now that I no longer exist?
What is this emptiness?" I shouted,
pointing at the void. "Is that hole
going to be meaningful for you forever?"
I turned away and left the room.

When and how do we become ourselves?
Is it when someone sees all the holes
between our life's bright points and appreciates
the gaps, the places we've fallen short, yet
comprehends how far light must travel
to enter our small eyes trying to piece together
the seen and unseen?

(continued)

I stared at the light opening through the space,
the light of who I am in all my empty, open potential.

Father didn't want me in his story any longer.
He'd created space for a different life for me
where I could be other than his version
of my story, could decide where my plot
might lead, and whether I wanted him in it.

Decades past that moment now, when I look
at the night sky, I think of that hole my father cut—
a gift he didn't know he gave.

Despite the grief, the loss,
it granted me a new life.

To that I say, "Thank you."

WHY AUGUST LEFT EDRA

Custer, South Dakota, 1943
August, age 62, Adah's sister's husband

Because no one was near to help
when our second child was born, Edra
described to our oldest daughter Freida
what to do and gave birth.

Edra wrapped rags around Gene's feet
to wear inside his shoes where the bottom
had worn through so he could walk
to school despite the holes.

When we opened the cured ham
my brother Neman sent, we discovered
maggots. Edra cut the maggots out,
and we ate the ham.

If the boys didn't get up in the morning
when Edra called, she might throw
a bucket of water on them
without remorse.

When Edra spotted an attractive horse
a Lakota owned, though he didn't want
to sell it, she sat with our son Cedric
at the man's circle, trying her best to bargain.

Until employment dried up, Edra and I worked
on Swan's Two-Bar Ranch. Then crickets
devoured crops across the state.

We moved from place to place, looking
for work during ongoing drought.

Farmers plowed their fields to plant wheat,
only to lose crops and soil to the wind.
Edra's strawberry hair went white.

(continued)

We persevered, though work was hard to find.
I got jobs in the sugar mills then the mica mine.
Edra worked outside, milked sheep, fed the horse,
hauled and carried water, cooked and washed
for the family. Our food most often was potatoes.
Only potatoes. We could afford them.
Edra served them cooked in lard,
and the nine of us ate.

This was our life.

Despite her hardness, I admired Edra's
tenacity, perseverance, and her
godawful stubborn will.

Edra and I fought often. A combat
of piercing words and invectives,
the children crouching in the other room
of our two-room house waiting
for the battle to end.

But the night Edra pulled out the iron skillet
and hit me on the head, I staggered, fell,
then crawled to my feet
and walked away.

I turned once to look at her
standing in the kitchen's bewildered light,
skillet still clenched in her angry hand,
but her face distraught, forlorn.

No resolution for the anger,
though I loved her.

I hesitated

but didn't return.

EDRA'S RIDE

Custer, South Dakota, 1943
Edra, age 48, Adah's sister

It was our last fight. August left.
Too many wounds we couldn't move past.

I needed to ride, get on my horse and go.
    I needed wind rushing over me,
        needed to know I wouldn't be crushed
            by my own anger,
                the fear of what might lie ahead.

I saddled Tony and rode off, muscled body pushing
for the horizon.
        His hooves beat the earth like a drum,
           roared into the cloud clotted sky,
               shook loose my thoughts'
               ragged thunder.

Smell of horse sweat.
    Cracked sky, rush of wind,
        scent of grass.
We ran and ran until the clouds broke and shattered
    into rain piercing the earth in ten million points.

I halted the horse. Dismounted.

What did I do when I struck August?
What have we done?
Not just August and me.
Every damn human being.
We break each other.
Ranch owners rich as kings, have laws
and loopholes to protect them.
For the rest there are storm clouds.
Rain.

(continued)

August worked in a mica mine
for a wage our family couldn't live on.
Adah sent the children shoes when we
couldn't afford them.
We ate that horrible worm-ridden ham
Neman sent because we had nothing else.

Moving, moving, and moving again,
renting houses with roofs that leaked,
August took whatever work available
until a tree fell on his back and broke it.
We break the earth, and it breaks us.

Wind cried as it raked the pines, rain
unhinged from the clouds, clattered to earth.

I sunk to the ground, let the downpour
of the whole unbearable poverty of every broken thing
soak through my hair,
my clothes,
my skin.

Mud pooled at my feet.
I lifted a stone from the earth.
Rose quartz. Its weight solid, firm
but its color soft.

I belong to the soil, am earth—
have to rise like the grass,
like trees,
and carry on.

WISHING

Cheyenne, Wyoming, 1944
Adah, age 55

Father had his wide-brimmed hat that sheltered him
from sand, rain, and too much sun.
Mother had her six-foot height to give her strength,
enabling her to talk down to most anyone.

For my sisters Edra and Jamie, their clothing
was their protection. Very few times in their adult lives
did they put on a dress. They wore men's shoes,
shirts, and overalls, did men's work,
wanted their respect.

My childhood employer Mrs. Hughes
had her perfume, other women their lipstick or rouge.
For some it's their strong voice,
others their horse or house.
Everyone has their methods of power,
defense and protection.

People say I'm tightfisted, spiteful, and cold,
but I don't have great beauty, wealth,
or social position.

In childhood I loved wildflowers scattered
like treasure among the wheat, the sky's blue field,
the balloons of cloud, rocky buttes, buzzing insects,
the earth's wet scent after rain, and finding a fossil
poking up from stony ground. These are gifts
not meant for power.

I know how to rope a cow, clean people's untidy
messes, and sew things up tight.
There's a multitude of human chaos, a lot
needing to be sewn closed. It is a tight world,
and I, too, am tight.

(continued)

I've hoarded food in my freezer for decades,
kept barrels full of sheets from the commissary
in the basement, and argued with my sisters
over every little thing because small things
are often of big importance.
Little things matter.

I hold close the shame I carry
for other people's actions—weights they hold
and can't release, that make me the prisoner.

I don't know how to let go.

I want to lean into the wind, to lie back
and laugh the way the earth laughs
when the wind slips through its grassy threads—
all their thin edges that twist, turn, thrash
but harm nothing,
only offer the vision of their rippled gold
to whoever gives them attention.

I've paid attention to my father,
to my husbands, to the laws that blind
and bind, and to unspoken restrictions
that sought to undo me.

Like the potato beetle and the grasshoppers' craving,
I'm forever hungry. Elizabeth Cady Stanton,
Susan B. Anthony, the Cheyenne, and the Crow—
by many they're seen as hostile.
Maybe they're just hungry, starving from all
that has been taken away or never permitted,
puzzled about how to feed their longing
to live a life different from the one allowed.

My story goes back so far there's no way
to find its beginning or discover its end.
Where could I locate a shovel to dig up the earth
hiding that foundation stone?

Inside my tight fist, underneath what people
have read as grasping, cold, uncaring, and mean,
is a brittle woman, broken so many times
I hold myself hard like stone, but precious,
like sapphire.

Yes. I want to be noble like my name's meaning,
to open my arms to it all, let go the tightness
holding me in and back and tell
my complete story.
But there's no lipstick, hat or horse
can help me do any of that.

Nine

Wind
1945–1952

BUILDING BRIDGES

Cheyenne, Wyoming, 1945
Leith, age 59, Adah's brother

The plains touch the sky, a thin thread drawing
the world together in a horizontal line of rest.

Today the sun rises to the end of World War II.
At last.

What was destroyed and what remains
is yet uncertain.

When I was a teacher, my students didn't
start their day with the pledge of allegiance.

It wasn't adopted until after the US entered the War.
Though a teacher no longer, I wish for a class

to discuss the significance of the American Frontier—
our desire to annex territory and expand borders,

would like to examine together whether Germany's
ambitions during the war reflect any of our own

country's history. To form this nation, leaders
broke contracts and lives, purposefully

denied justice and freedom.
My work today is to build bridges.

Since the War is over, I wonder what foundations
will now hold us, what actions span the gaps in ideals?

Will the millions who died in the War, the innocents
singled out who were feared and intimidated—

those who died because they were different,
be enough to help us remember what happens

when leaders say only they have the answers,
that their power is what matters?

My father loved control.
In his house I learned domination doesn't

build a bridge strong enough
to cross between worlds.

I've lived on a prairie all my life.
Others live with mountains.

Settlers plowed and removed the prairie's grass,
were encouraged to rid the countryside of natives.

How do we define borders yet listen
and look beyond them, build bridges

that allow us to stretch beyond fear and possession?
How do we become one nation, use tensions

as support, create a causeway of freedom and justice
that unifies us all?

WHY DID I MARRY YOU?
DRAFT FOR AN ANNIVERSARY LETTER

Mesa, Arizona, 1953
Litton, age 57, Adah's third husband

Because though I'd been through the War
    even as we were headed for another,
      it wasn't an obstacle to your commitment.

Because though there are Americans who suspected
    those of German ancestry could be spies,
    and German language was erased
    from schools and street names, though our
    president said he "stood against
    every form of hyphenated American,"
    called it "a dagger,"
    you appreciate my heritage.

Because you iron my wrinkles smooth, understand
    the ways people try and name me
    isn't the whole of who I am.

Because, dear woman, unlike the young woman
    I was set to marry, you were older, experienced,
    willing to move to unknown places.
    You're tenacious, exacting, take command
    of your work and know how to survive.

Because you can turn a head, a sheet, know how
    to tumble a man and make a fine bed.

Because of the way you fold the dough for apple pie
    and ask me to listen to morning's birds.

Because I was married before, have been with
    numerous women, and you accept that.

Because of your love for perfectly white napkins.

Because your eyes turned wide as roses when I
    brought you wildflowers—hyssop, yarrow,
    paintbrush, as if they were the gift you'd waited for
    for years.

Because your presence is water that washes
    hidden wounds that allows me to look spotless,
    though you know I'm not.

Because you welcomed me into your arms as if
    a blessing.

Because you are the near and the far of what I reach for
    in the middle of the night, the prayer
    I don't know how to say.

Because even though you're bullheaded and stubborn,
    you are good to me.

THE TREES

North Little Rock, Arkansas, 1946
Adah, age 57

A short time ago this town held four thousand
German prisoners of war. Things are calmer now,
thankfully, so this morning Litton and I
drove around Little Rock to explore Autumn.

Sweet gums at the capitol dressed themselves
in topaz and copper. Maples on riverbanks
huddled together beneath red and amber blankets.
Up north, oaks wore suits of rust.

The cold that brings these gifts of color is a sign
the trees soon will lose all they hold.
Seems I should feel sorrow standing beneath
their branches, knowing their loss grows daily,
but the War is over, and it's my birthday.
Mostly, I feel embraced.

I'm a woman of the prairies and open skies.
When I speak, my accent tells the story:
I'm an outsider here.
Sugar maples, hickory, dogwood, and gum—
trees in general are foreign to me.
My history is from a different world,
one made of grass.

Life here has comforts I enjoy.
Same as for others who live nearby,
Litton and I have electricity, indoor toilets,
heat, a toaster, refrigerator, and a radio.
Now and then, though, I take off my shoes,
walk barefoot to remember what it feels like.

Every place has something important
it wants to tell us.

In spring, Little Rock's magnolias lift
their flowers like cups to gather the afternoon's
blue, and redbuds grow blossoms on their trunks.
In fall we ride roads curling through trees aflame
with brilliant color. Still, sometimes I wish
to hear the fields of prairie grass sigh
when the wind moves through.
I long for its voice
whispering in my ear.

Arkansas isn't my forever home, but likely
I'll miss people's accents, sweet tea,
and the city's abundant trees when I leave.

All of us in the family, including Mama, Father,
their parents and great grandparents too—everyone
left the land they were born on, and I have too.
Don't know if I'll ever return to Nebraska
or will want to.
For now, I carry my home with me,
choose the parts to keep.

Today I stood beside the river
in the afternoon's gold light, opened
my arms to a maple's leafy blaze,
and made my birthday wish:
to be like these trees—
the way they allow their beauty to burn
and burn and yet don't die, even after
losing all that allowed them
to live into their fullness,
even as every colorful leaf
drifts down to earth.

IN THE PLAINS OF WIND

Newcastle, Wyoming, 1947
Lenore, age 64, Adah's sister

When Jed died, I stayed with Jamie for a time,
but now live near Margot in Newcastle, a town
built at the end of the Burlington train tracks

for railroad workers, cowboys and Cambria's
coal miners, later expanding its borders
for oil-refinery workers.

No horse carts roll down the road today.
Just cars on the streets and traffic lights.
Years ago, I worked at a restaurant here.

Met and married Jed here too.
Never imagined I'd move back,
but Newcastle's home now.

Margot was a wild child. Didn't want
to be told what to do. Cooking, sewing,
tending a garden—the things that made

me happy bored her but made Jed
more aware, me more patient.
Margot is restless, likes action.
We're different.

Though adopted, she's my child.
I want to be near her. The plains
are full of wind, a place of constant shifting.

I don't know the story of what pushed
those born before me to leave their homes,
but no one seems to have stayed put.

Still, I find it difficult to leave a place I've called
home—allow the wind to shape and reshape me
as I let go one life for another.

There are many things I've not seen or done,
as well as things I couldn't change.
Everyone has their poverties.

I'm little more than rain evaporating from grass,
a scent in the air that disappears.
I'll not live much longer, but served

God knows how many meals to Jed and Margot,
hundreds of pies too. I lived long enough
to sense my husband's heart grow wise,

and Margot gain focus.
No more carrying water for a bath
or chopping wood to cook.

Music floods my radio's wires now.
I've absorbed decades of bird song,
witnessed meadows stirred with ceaseless wind,

endured blizzards I didn't think I'd survive.
I was a mother to Margot.

That isn't nothing.

NOT JUST ANOTHER MORNING

Little Rock, Arkansas, 1948
Adah, age 59

Morning's light peeked through the blinds.
The aroma of brewed coffee warmed the air.
"Excellent!" I said when Litton told me
Truman signed the bill stating women
can join the military now. "But they can't
serve in combat!" he exclaimed, newspaper
spread across the table as I entered the door.

"Women served as clerks, nurses, pilots,
translators, and mechanics during the War.
You know that! Truman did the smart thing."

I flung back the room's curtains,
let the light flood in.

"The laundry women at the base
will jump at the opportunity to enlist.
They deserve the opportunity
and pay."

"It'll weaken the forces!" Litton insisted
as he sipped his coffee. "What man would
want to take orders from a woman?
Men on military bases have paid them for sex
since forever. Who'll believe a woman
in the military actually served the country?"
he emphasized. "It won't be better for them
when they get out either. People will assume
they've entertained men for years
and got paid for it."

I sat at the table, let the light
fall across my whole body.

"Women know what side their bread
is buttered on. They've taken orders
for years. They'll know what to do."

"Pour me a cup of coffee, won't you?" I asked.
He lifted his eyebrow.
"Bring me a slice of toast, too.
I like it with jelly."

ROCK HUNTING

Cheyenne, Wyoming, 1949
Leith, age 63, Adah's brother

A dirt-caked Buick rolls down the road alongside
a polished Packard, Cadillac, and a Pontiac.
Avery and I drive past the courthouse headed north
to hunt for agate, poke around for jasper, fossils—
whatever treasure might appear.
Avery loves the search.

As our family learned, stony earth made ploughing
difficult when prairie land was first turned
for farming. The days of horse-drawn ploughs
are done. Same company that made tanks
and artillery for the War makes tractors.
Now the War's over, people are moving to cities.
Tractors and migrant workers keep farmwork going.

The Swan Ranch our family worked for
is selling off their holdings. Ranches everywhere
have trouble now. Ranches are getting bigger,
farmers fewer. People now grow single crops,
use irrigation systems, pesticides, herbicides,
and machinery to make a go of farming.

Our sister Jamie's got a machine to do the wash
at Fort Warren in Cheyenne. Adah's got one
in Arkansas. Machine or no machine, work today
is mostly about production.

Back in '36, I watched Charlie Chaplin
in *Modern Times* fail to keep up with his task
at a conveyor belt while attempting to chase away
a fly. Difficult to chase a dream as well these days
while keeping up with one's vocation.

But not for Avery. It could be the fourth of July,
everyone excited about firework explosions
or a rodeo. What he looks forward to, even while
at work with a plough, is the hunt for stones.
For Avery, they aren't obstructions in the field,
they're the possibility of amazement.

After miles of flatland and shrubs, we climb
from the car to inhale the earth's rich scent.
The ground stuffed with stones like chips
in a cookie, buckets in hand, we comb the earth
looking for agates' lacy plumes, snail shaped
fossils, red jasper, and petrified wood.

No specific purpose needed when rock hunting.
No timeline or agenda to fulfill, just walking
the land with the possibility of reaching
into the soil to find something formed
several million years ago that waited
another million before we touched it—
something solid, beautiful,
and unrelated to any need
for productivity.

DEFINITIONS

Cheyenne, Wyoming, 1950
Jamie, age 53, Adah's sister

Father treated women like good workhorses,
    a necessary and practical choice
    for carrying on life.

Mother believed women are rivers
    capable of bending and turning,
    able to flow over any terrain.

My sisters considered themselves wind,
    strong, persistent, and moving consistently
    to lower pressure.

My brothers thought of women as trees,
    shade-givers in a dry land
    where few trees thrive.

The women at the laundry considered themselves earth,
    soft, deep, and necessary,
    eroded and used for grazing,
    longing for renewal.

The women working at the hotel saw themselves
    as coal, a source of fuel that generated power,
    as an engine, creating movement
    toward a longed-for destination,
    as salt, a valued element
    able to preserve.

Edra's oldest daughter Freida quotes Proverbs'
    description of Wisdom:
        "She is a reflection of the eternal light,
        untarnished mirror of God's active power,
        and image of all goodness."

I am a plow. I work in fields, turn hard soil, bury weeds.

Merriam Webster's dictionary offers a definition
of womankind as "a servant or attendant."
    She may be.

A woman may be any of these definitions.
All the ways used to define a woman,
or that she uses to define herself—
    Wisdom defies them,
      says she is more.

SOMETHING ABOUT ASH

Little Rock, Arkansas, 1952
Adah, age 63

Winter, and people are using their fireplaces
and wood stoves again. Though central heat
is now available, my neighbors still burn wood.
I can't bear the smoke, though winter could be
worse in Wyoming with horrific winds, ten-foot
snow drifts, frigid temperatures, and thousands
of dead cattle like they had in '49.

I long for open space.
Sky.
Got to get in the car, leave
this crowded neighborhood,
turn on the radio and ride.

Lightnin' Hopkins plays "War News Blues,"
singing "sad news every day... Mama
what shall we do?"
He's talking to me.

News comes on.
Men in congress are asking people
to tell things they've done
or shouldn't have,
while Litton works to make sure
enough fuel, food, flamethrowers, carbines,
boots, and bazookas get delivered to Korea.

I want to roll the windows
down, want wind
     swirling around me,
something fresh
to brush through my hair.

But street after street
smoke
rises from chimneys.

I keep the windows shut and drive on.
Don't want to breathe that air.

The Sunshine Boys' voices follow the news.
"People start prayin'," they sing,
and I do.
My Chevy glides down the road as if a bird—
not a crow or common sparrow, but a sandhill crane
with wide wings, long legs trailing through air
above the plain along the river.

Arkansas isn't home.
Been here too long. I ache
for the Wyoming wind.
Smell of grass.
The sky.

Linton's military career grew from his belief
in freedom and the desire to belong.
America is built on that wish.
Three wars he's served in now.

There's what a person wants to give.
Then there's the things we don't understand
that break a person
because of that same love.

When young, I dreamed to own a shop
selling flowers and linens. I've let that fade.
Where I can go is connected to roads that exist,
the maps I'm given and can read.

Like those who McCarthy questions,
I have stories I'd rather others didn't know.
I follow the rules of the road,
but there's a world beyond marked lines—

(continued)

other air, places without smoke
even if I don't live in them.

Far enough away from the city now
to escape the smoky haze, I stop the car,
get out to gaze into the web of lights beyond.

A star falls. A dream
blazes through the lush dark
then fizzles out.

I need to forgive myself
for the things I've wished for
but can't change.

Ten

Mending
1953–1965

A SLOW FULLNESS

Chugwater, Wyoming, 1953
Avery, age 60, Adah's brother

"For cryin' out loud, you're as slow as molasses
in January." How many times had I heard
someone tell me that?

Sure, I could spin on the dance floor,
but I'm not like others. It's not a secret.
Never was good at school.
I didn't cry about being slow, though.

While others burrowed into mines
to cut coal, calculated numbers, or hauled
stone for railroad bed, I've risen each day to light
spilled across fields, clouds lazing by.

Sixty years I've walked this earth.
Despite its drought and ice, despite a world
rattled in war's despair, and jolts from aging bones
as I bump along gravel roads, I inhale
the wheat's slow ripening as it rustles
the sky's fine blue fabric.

Every day the world ripples with wind.
Grit mixes with cloud.
There's no need to forgive myself
for what I couldn't change.
I've received my daily bread.

I pick a few wheat kernels,
rub them in my hand.

It's a good world to give myself to.

WHAT JAMIE WAITED TO HEAR

Cheyenne, Wyoming, 1953
Jamie, age 56, Adah's sister

Howard, my first husband, was a tall man
with a small heart. I married him
because I was alone and didn't want to be.

A temperamental man, Howard believed
in signs. If a raven flew overhead, someone
was going to die. When a neighbor found
a dinosaur bone in his field, something dangerous
was sure to come our way.
Usually, that was Howard yelling,
throwing things, angry at what he wanted
and didn't get.

He thought he wanted me.
But I saw the signs and divorced him,
a story with an ending he didn't like.

My second husband, Frank, liked horses,
and worked with me on the ranch,
but fell in love with cigarettes, alcohol,
and the company of other women.
I divorced him, too.

My third husband, Alfred, loved farming
but let me do the work. I didn't mind too much.
He smoked less, didn't yell often or drink every day
and stayed around in the evenings.

Belonging. That's a strange word.
To belong to someone or they to you.
I've spent a lot of time longing, longing to be
someone to somebody.

(continued)

None of my husbands have said the words, "I love you."
Neither do I say them.
So hard to say what I've scarcely experienced or heard.

When I did hear them one summer evening
sitting under stars with Alfred, instead of telling him
I loved him too, I suddenly grew silent,
absorbing the light shooting from a falling star,
its unasked brilliance plummeting across
night's violet dark.

Nothing had ever seemed so beautiful
or so brief.

LISTENING LONG AND FAR

Mesa, Arizona, 1957
Adah, age 68

I was doing laundry, scrubbing stains from
last night's napkins when Litton came in with news
from Arkansas, "Governor Orval Faubus surrounded
Little Rock's Central High School with the National Guard."
Litton opened the paper and read, "Soldiers, armed
with rifles and carbines, turned back nine Negro students."

I put down the napkins and took up the paper showing
Elizabeth Eckford in her crisp, clean clothes walking
away from the crowd that pushed her along, and the girl
behind her with the scrunched-up vinegar face,
bared teeth, and lips curled into a snarl.
That girl's warped face pierced me.

I looked up from the paper to gaze through
the window remembering cactus' sharp spines,
how I once accidentally backed into one
and it took a pair of pliers to remove its barb.

The steadfast set of Elizabeth's face
is what sticks with me most, the small furrow
in her brow above her dark glasses, her head
tilted slightly down, watching where she's going.

I don't know Elizabeth's story,
but recognize the look of a woman
silently holding herself together
beneath what can't be said.

It's not just today's angry crowd that girl
suffers from. She's moving into history's
windstorm when trying to enter that school—
a cyclone, a hurricane, a blowing over
of the million little rocks men mortared together
and are used to standing on.

(continued)

People can demand control, bring out their
armed guards, their tractors and chemicals,
make the world we live in a giant factory, can
process people through a convoluted system.
They can storm and shout, show up as vigilante
crowds with their curses, guns and rope.

But people like Elizabeth don't do things solely
to keep their days happy. They do things
because beneath a desert's angry heat
and the rigid rock weight of hard-hearted rules, life
begs to break through and rise from dry soil
with the surprise of color from land
believed to be barren.

How she's able to walk through the crowd's mass
of churning ire, I don't know, except that her vision
must be as expansive as the sky, clear
as the water that streamed from the rock
Moses struck to slake the thirst
of multitudes.

I've traveled into the desert here
outside Mesa where I now live, sat
on a slab of sandstone and listened
long and far to the land's
deep silence.

The sky's expansive blue settles over me.
A wordless voice
drifts down
gentle
     as a feather—
says Earth
     is borderless
          belongs to itself.
Holds everyone.

I'm old, worn as a sandstone slab.
Don't have Elizabeth's courage
to walk through doors I've never entered,
but ache for the strength of a spring desert flower
to stand like Elizabeth, the open petals of her humanity
set on absorbing the warmth of the day's full sun.

SWEET DAYS

Mesa, Arizona, 1958
Adah, age 69

Mesa's summer sun seared the land and turned
the distant mountains red.

After Litton retired from the military at Williams Field,
we stayed on in Arizona for time to wander through
its chaparral with abandoned mines, towns—land
bristled with saguaro and prickly pears.

But it was a pleasure leaving summer's heat
to travel to California and ride the country roads
east of San Diego that led to Edra's oldest
daughter's house, sun floating down
to brush the hillside's yellow grass.

How satisfying to stand in Freida's yellow kitchen
and show her how to make noodles for soup.
How happy to greet her four year old girl
named after me who likes to ride her trike,
and laughs while standing on her head.

I'm sixty-nine now, dear girl, but that's
what I want to do too—stand on my head,
greet the world upside down, let laughter's rivers
flow into my thoughts as if ruby jewels
from a pomegranate spilled into a bright bowl.

When I returned to Arizona, I sent young Adah
a t-shirt with a girl on the front who had large eyes
able to move in all directions, and writing below
that said, "I'm a little devil from Phoenix, Arizona."

I hope she wears the shirt when standing on her head
to discover the world from different angles, so whether
living in a forest or desert, surrounded by asphalt,

grassy fields or chunks of heavy stone, though
it's not the world she was born into, she can find
a way to greet all she sees.

An extension of her parents' lives and all who
came before, in my mind I see Freida's young
Adah, her body upside down, eyes a sparkle,
as head down against the davenport
she balances herself.

Her laughter tumbles into my chest,
wobbles there like jelly, says it's possible
to stand history and old failures on their heads
and become someone new.

EDRA SITS FOR A PHOTO

Custer, South Dakota, 1961
Edra, age 64, Adah's sister

My sisters Adah and Jamie persistently asked,
"Why are you having more children? One or two.
Isn't that enough? There are ways to stop, you know."

They would know, but I didn't ask.
Jamie's wild ways. Adah's history.
Children were a natural consequence of marriage.
I wanted to be with August but didn't want
to follow their advice.

I loved the outside, the farm and ranch life
with horses to ride and cows to feed.
I wore men's clothes, did men's work.
Childbirth prevention with herbs, chemicals,
some crazy, strange-fangled contraption, long-term
abstinence, or rubbers August would never
find or use—all the options seemed absurd.

So, I had children, seven of them—resulting in
moving from place to place struggling
to pay the rent, scrambling for food—months
and years of nothing but potatoes, and children
without proper clothing or shoes.

A woman needs determination and guts
to live in this world. I had to work,
and the children learned how to care for themselves,
same as I did.

Heat, winds that cut through the land as if a scythe,
floods, drought, blizzards, or seven children's lives
depending on you, you endure it all and keep going.

Today my oldest daughter Freida visiting
for August's funeral, brings me a dress to wear
and wants me to sit for a photo.
All that air against my legs, its silly, loose fabric
about my body. A dress feels too fragile,
too open.

I prefer the comfort and protection of bib overalls.
But to please Freida, I put on the dress
and sat for the photo—tried on
what it might be like to be a different woman.

Her name is my wish for her: Freida Evelyn,
a peaceful life. Maybe she will find a way
to wear a dress and still feel free
enough to be herself.

AFTER LITTON,
ADAH REFLECTS ON HER THIRD MARRIAGE

Mesa, Arizona, 1965
Adah, age 76

Kindness, tenderness, attention to mood or emotion,
romance—these were things of fantasy.
I'd never had them.
Wishing for them could bring disappointment.
Marriage was a practical move.

When I first met Litton, he was with a different woman.
I didn't see that as an obstacle.
I knew how to please a man
and wanted him.

Marriage is a negotiation of terms
partners agree to live with, and the terms
looked good to us.

As a widow, I had life insurance money and income
from Gerard's pension, as well as deeds to properties
held in collateral from loans to people
during the Depression. A military man, Litton
had guaranteed income, and I assumed
a good-sized pension. After years of uncertainty
in childhood about food and shelter, these
were the comfort and security I wanted.

So, we married. A simple ceremony.
No need for frills and extra expense.

Thirty years I spent with Litton.

He was good enough to me. It's true.
He could dance and make me smile.
We had a solid house, one like I'd always
wished for—a living room stuffed with matching
couch and chairs with plush cushions, lace tablecloths,

ceramic dinnerware, glass goblets, and linen napkins.
These gave me a kind of beauty I'd longed for.
True, Litton loved me, could make stars
shine between us, but there was a sediment
left in him from when he first fought in the War,
a silent grief that emerged from hidden shadows
to shake the stalks of grass he tried
to bury memories under.

Litton had given his life to the military—
wanted the shade of its structure and show
of might to ensure safety, security, freedom.
But tangled thoughts scrambled through his head
with no crater big enough to bury them in.

I didn't just marry a man I married his history too.
Shot off legs, bodies blasted into dust, nightmares
he returned from War with his first wife couldn't
hold up under—were these necessary losses?
He stepped around his doubts skillfully,
but never resolved them.

We moved to humid Arkansas, later to Arizona
with its dry, red hills. Always, I cooked his favorite
foods, did laundry as he liked: shirts pressed
wrinkle-free, collars ironed to a perfect point.
My house was tidy, orderly, and clean,
my clothes well-made.
I wanted the respect these brought.
But life was not much more than that.

When Litton died, I didn't take his pension.
Mine was better.

After the funeral, I sat alone in that desert-still
Arizona house filled with a wealth of goods
I'd wished to possess since childhood—
that dream's weight lying there stiff, stale,
coated with dust after returning from the burial
at Denver's Fort Logan.

(continued)

Kindness, an arm reaching toward me
in tenderness, in friendship—I wanted them.
All that beautiful dinnerware.
Stability.
Structure.
Respect.
They aren't enough.

I turned on the radio.
An orchestra was playing.
Violins rose in volume, swelling
like enormous billowing clouds, mounting
high into the heavens
ready to rain,
        then dissolving,
sky turning clear, only the quietest
of sighs present—a soft wind's wrinkle
on morning grass as the sun
                stretched to warm the world.
I'd never heard anything more able
to define my yearning—

At seventy-five years old, I realized
what I'd been wishing for all my life
but had no words for
was something more
like music.

A RETURN TO REFUGE, ADAH'S PLAN

Cheyenne, Wyoming, 1965
Adah, age 76

The house echoed with the memory
of Litton's firm voice,
and the absence of his voice
when he died.

For most of my life I've wished to belong.
With Litton gone, I recognized
I didn't belong to Arizona's desert scrub.

I belonged to the prairies.

I longed to watch Wyoming's wind-tides
flowing across seamless earth, expand
with wild bergamot's exhaled scent,
watch cottonwoods turn gold,
and immerse myself in the sky's
blue cascades
like I did when a child.

I'd return to Wyoming
to walk again through wheat fields.
Tassels tossed with sunset air beside me,
moon rising into the infinite heavens, I would unfold
with the pearl of its astonishing silence,
listen for how to begin anew.

Eleven

Quilt
1966–1983

THERE'S NOT ENOUGH SUGAR
IN THIS WORLD

Custer, South Dakota, 1966
Edra, age 71, Adah's sister

Though highways are being built across the nation,
my life hasn't changed much. I have electricity
and a car, but still live in a two-room house,
wondering where my life is going.

A world of things has gone awry since the day
I was born. Something I know, though, a lot
can feel better with a cut of cornbread, a glass
of root beer, and slice of gooseberry pie.

When he was president, FDR told us
"We have nothing to fear but fear itself."
But then there was World War II, an atomic bomb,
the Korean war, and the war in Vietnam.

Hippies today talk about love, though it seems
we're all a long way off from understanding
how to live or love.

In my family, my brothers' wives never had children
of their own. Family members adopted other family
members' children born outside of marriage.

As a single mother after August left, I kept working.
Motherhood isn't a necessary or ideal state for women.
Abortions or pregnancies from men who raped them,
my sisters made choices I didn't, though the children
born to them are likely glad enough.
They're alive, despite difficulty they've known.

Still, if it were available when they were young,
the pill could've reduced our family's poverty
and grief.

To feed families as well as our own selves
requires years of sweat and strength.

When I lived in Chugwater with August, I learned
Native tribes once drove animals over its rocky bluffs
for food. The sound buffalo made falling
into the water gave the town its name.
Though audible to no one else, hidden hooves
rumble against my gut, a clattering wildness
inside my body, thrashing beneath my veins' rivers,
chugging and colliding against the rocks of my bones
for unnamed food I've craved but rarely received.

My sister Jamie feeds her dog sugar.
Six teaspoons a day.
I feed myself sugar, my diabetes
often out of control.
I didn't get much sweetness in life.
Now I overdo it. Can't help myself.

A lot of things can be mended
with a cut of cornbread, a glass of root beer,
and a slice of gooseberry pie.
Love isn't one of them.
There's never enough in the world.

Except sometimes.

PATCHWORK

Cheyenne, Wyoming, 1966
Adah, age 77

My niece Freida arrived from California today
with her daughters, curly haired Sofia,
and my namesake—twelve-year-old Adah,
her hair turned up in a flip.

After more than a thousand miles on a Greyhound bus
they smelled like cigarettes, but I was glad to see them.

Adah's thin and short for her age, has long fingers.
"Perfect for playing the piano," I say, observing
her open face as she sits next to her mother
on the chair's soft arm. She's the same age I was
when Jacob Hughes raped me. I use that word now
that I couldn't say back then.

A gentle girl, I'm glad young Adah's world
is different than mine was. Her parents
don't need to send her to work.
She goes to school instead, can explore
her dreams. I'll never learn to swim,
won't fly on an airplane, or go to college.
But someday she might.

Young Adah will likely break rules I had to follow
as a child. Probably will break rules
she grew up with too.

I remember my sister Jamie's anger when years ago
she roared at me, "There's things more important
than rules, Adah!" I'm old but still trying to listen
inside my bones to know what's important.

I need glasses to see now, got a double chin as well.
My body's moving slow. Guess falling apart
is what allows a person to finish growing up.

I've got a patchwork life. It's taking time
to remake and become myself.
Some things were torn from my life. Others
I cut away myself. But I'm piecing things together
to create something new. I wish that for every Adah
and Sofia too.

MARGOT'S DISCOVERY

Newcastle, Wyoming, 1967
Margot, age 59, Adah's, and Lenore and Jed's daughter

After teaching for forty years, I retired,
hoped to travel to Mexico, and needed a copy
of my birth certificate to apply for a passport.

A wave of joy welled up in me when
the clerk at city hall handed me my copy.
Glancing down the document, my eyes stumbled
on the words "Illegitimate."
I choked.
The room felt suddenly cold, the walls
claustrophobic. But there was no escape
from what I'd read.

I wasn't who I thought I was.
Neither were my parents.
I believed I knew them, yet never glimpsed
the truth inside their eyes.

Who was I?

This wasn't like teaching math
where numbers have precise values
and problems are solved with clearly defined answers.

Families adopted each other's illegitimate children.
I'd known that, but never guessed
one of those children was me.

When teaching geography, I explained how
invisible lines created boundaries
and defined countries.

I didn't need a passport to go somewhere new.
In a single moment I'd crossed an invisible boundary,
was lost to the mystery of my own origin.

I drifted out to the parking lot, sat in my car,
birth certificate loose in my open palms,
and mindlessly watched a cottonwood's leaves
rotate with the wind. I turned my eyes from
the tree to the sky, and thought of my son, Everett.

Neither of us knew our great-grandparents.
Quiet morning bird calls, seasons of wind
and snow, the earth's deep stillness sinking
into bones—the land has nurtured and shaped him,
as well as me. Many raise us into who we become.

No need, I decided, to alter my dream of travel.
This was the perfect time to journey
through an unfamiliar country.
Like unseen stars in the day-lit sky, all origins
reach somewhere beyond sight or understanding.

HANGING LAUNDRY

Cheyenne, Wyoming, 1971
Adah, age 82

Some are stepping out in their platform shoes
this afternoon, getting on airplanes.
This evening Walter Cronkite will deliver
the TV news, but I'm focused
on getting my washing done.

I pull damp clothes from the laundry basket,
grateful for a washing machine, glad
it's no longer necessary to bend
and scrub half the day, or half a life
like when I was young. There's other ways
to get things clean.

The wind blows as I lift underclothes
from my basket remembering my early days,
the shame that has followed me like a shadow.

The laundry women I supervised, who made
money on the side as prostitutes, and the women
I managed at the hotel's brothel.
Why should I still feel the taint of that work?
I pin the underwear to the line.
"Enough of that," I say.
"Finished."

I raise my dresses from the basket,
drape them over my arm.
That I didn't have proper clothes
or shoes when younger, didn't have
the correct manners or accent for places
I moved to, that I couldn't come up with
the right words when I needed them
to avoid a fight—enough of that too.
I press the dresses' shoulder seams
to the line and hang each one.

That Claude was already married when he married me.
That my husbands have died and I am alone.
That Jacob and Jed thought they had the God-given
right to my body because they were men.

That I never claimed as mine
the girl I gave birth to.

Washcloths, tablecloths, sheets,
everything's up on the line now.
The basket is empty.
I'm done with the disgrace.
Don't want to be washing it
and washing it
anymore.

My parents, the grandparents I never met,
great-grandparents too—it's not just my laundry
that needs to be done, is it?
It's everybody's.
We're all part of this fabric.

Drought wheezing over the land.
Snows storming down in a white blind.
For God's sake,
I don't have to listen to Walter Cronkite
or get on an airplane to recognize the Earth itself
is falling apart and being made and remade
every day. Nothing is complete.
Why should I expect my life
to be different?

I tell myself all the reasons
but the heart
wants something different.

The heart says, "Let go.
The wind will do its work now.

Let it be."

CEDRIC MEETS WITH ADAH AND JAMIE

Cheyenne, Wyoming, 1972
Cedric, age 73, Adah's brother

When I lived in Cheyenne, my sisters
Adah and Jamie lived there too.
Years went by but we never met.

After Della's death at our home in Colorado,
I came to Cheyenne, rode with Edra's daughter
to Jamie's house to visit. Adah sat on her chair's edge,
back straight, legs crossed, hands folded.
Jamie leaned back into the sofa,
gazed at the walls.

The room needs more windows, I thought,
remembering the house's stark walls
where we grew up, the light there taut
and stale enough to choke on.

Della's death and our family's past
was too painful to discuss.
Lenore and Leith died some time back,
Edra and Avery recently.
The residue of loss hung in the air like dust.
What was there to say?

Before retirement, I inspected banks' records,
calculated their risks, ensured whether it was safe
for people to deposit money there, my aim
to provide assurance amidst adversity.
But if scrutinized, the ground we stand on
gives no certainty. Our family has known that
as a fundamental fact for years.

Some of the family's choices were better than others.
The family moving to Cheyenne those years ago
improved our opportunities.

In the past, fights in Wyoming over ownership
between cattle ranchers and sheepherders
went on for ages.

Drops in coal and oil prices, government scandals,
unemployment—I see now these aren't disconnected
from our own struggles and diminishments.

The edge of hunger, divorce, death—
we've experienced them all.
How to hold the sum of our sorrows
loosely enough to step beyond them,
that's the difficulty.

The best we could do that visit
was to sit with each other in silence,
holding what we know and have shared
before needing to go our separate ways.

A CAT COMES TO ADAH

Cheyenne, Wyoming, 1972
Adah, age 83

Living by myself for years now and getting old,
I wake to the day's routines—cleaning, preparing food.

My life, my parents' life, those of grandparents
and great-grandparents I've never known—

all of us. Breath goes in, goes out, in, out,
and then we disappear.

We're here, walking to the post office perhaps,
then a tremendous wind rises, scours the prairie,

and, as if mere dust, we blow away into the current
of a great unknown.

Peering out my window each day into the far horizon,
I see plains filling my vision with their spaciousness.

I wanted to be a hill people had to go around
or climb over to get where they wanted to go.

But I know I'm really a single grass strand
in a vast prairie.

My roots go into deep earth,
but I won't last long.

I'll become nameless like everyone else.
I've spent years saving, measuring, calculating

values and worth through crises and depressions.
Then a cat appeared in my yard unexpectedly

one October day. She waited at my door,
her mouth opening in a near voiceless meow

when I noticed her sitting there, hoping
to receive food. I hadn't wanted a cat,

but she'd chosen me and remained in the yard,
day after day, returning to my door.

I invited her into the house, but she'd stay
only a few moments before panicking

and dashing for the door, then waited there outside,
as if longing to come in.

Eventually, she let me brush my hand across
her back. Fur the color of cocoa or toffee, softer

than velvet, I fed her every day and hoped
she'd stay, but at the movement of a chair

she'd dart across the floor and out the door.
Then, one evening months later, she sat on my lap

for half an hour without wanting to escape
while I petted her behind the ears and under the chin.

At last, she'd given me her trust.
I'm not alone now. Sable sits beside me

every evening, luxuriating in passing time together,
and any strokes that come her way.

She sleeps for hours, cleans her fur, eats,
and never worries about her hair turning gray

or what I think of her. I watch her and wonder,
what have I known of peaceful living?

Most my life, I've wanted to be more or different
than I was, passing on my disapproval to others.

I've argued with my husbands over the correct
pronunciation of names and locations of streets.   *(continued)*

I've criticized my sister Jamie about her choice
of partner, harped on my sister Edra

for the weight she'd gained, condemned her
for having so many children.

I've sneered at the color of gloves
women chose to wear.

Yes, I've been this woman to others
as well as to myself.

I have a thousand inconsistencies.

Being strong, beautiful, in charge, right—
none of that matters to a cat.

When sleeping, Sable's paw rests
calmly on her eye. She seeks no fault

in anything.
Evenings on the davenport, her quiet body

beside me, I stroke her soft pelt.
Time envelops me,

and I expand into its grace,
along with the incompleteness

of everything I've known.

QUILT

Cheyenne, Wyoming, 1973
Adah, age 84

No longer in my house, I live at a home for the elderly
where I'm slowly stitching together a quilt
for my great niece, Adah. Edra's daughter Freida
named her after me.

Home from college, she wrote to ask about my life.
What words could I find to describe my story?
It's difficult to tell it to myself.

"My life is like your mother's," I wrote her.
I know it's not an answer she wants.
Mother, grandmother, daughter, or great-niece—
isn't there a thread running through every
woman's life similar to my story?

As I sew, I recall the day my sisters and I lassoed
a steer. We'd seen the animal's unpredictable
moves, and had practiced perfecting our timing.

Eyes focused on the target, loop sailing above the head,
rope reeling through Jamie's hands, she dropped it
over the steer's head, Edra pulled up the slack
as its head jerked back and the animal
fell to the ground.

Together, we held the ropes that kept the steer in place.
Muscles strained and tense, tugging on the ropes,
I looked in the steer's eyes as it bellowed
and struggled in the dirt trying to free itself,
and saw myself pulling against restraints,
resisting the rules and life I'd been given
that held me tight. Then I thought of us sisters,
ropes in hand, each of us working to hold on
to a life we wanted.

(continued)

Thinning hair, stiff joints and sagging skin,
no longer strong like that steer we roped,
I still hold on.

If before I had beauty, it's gone now.
A woman is never pleasing enough
in someone's eyes, though my niece
doesn't follow my generation's rules for beauty.
She's got a short, lopsided haircut
and her own priorities, but believes me beautiful
because that's how her mother sees me.

I never owned a shop selling fabric or flowers
like I imagined when young, but I've made
plenty of quilts. Stitch by stitch I piece together
this one now with bright colored squares
between strips of flowered fabric, a story of cloth
I make with my hands from clothes I've worn.

Slowly, the quilt comes together, a pattern
reaching back through time and the long thread
of unnamed women whose lives we'll never know
who patched together what they had so they could
pass on something beautiful to bring a bit of warmth.

MOON LANDING, MINI SKIRTS, AND OTHER TRANSFORMATIONS

Cheyenne, Wyoming, 1978
Adah, age 89

From the astonishment of the moon landing,
astronauts sending images of Earth floating
as if a bubble, to "free love," protests and the pill,
to a child conceived in a test-tube, today's world
is little like the one I was born into.

But I'm not convinced love is ever free.

Since my niece Riva's divorce, she works
in an office as well as keeps the house organized,
and cooks meals. Riva's got spark.
"If I ever had a daughter," I've told her,
"I'd want her to be like you."

I gave birth to a girl, Margot, but
my sister Lenore fed and clothed her.
Margot was her and Jed's adopted daughter.
I never claimed Margot as mine.

Change was exotic when the circus came
to Cheyenne in '33 with camels and elephants
trailing two miles up Snyder Avenue.
The spectacle transported us out of the mundane
into a place floating with magic.

Though not exotic like the circus, today's changes
astonish. Women can choose to work, have a child,
or decide to remain unmarried.
There's hundreds of ways a woman might
give herself to the world now. None of the choices
appeared like magic.

(continued)

Nowadays, a woman can wear make-up
or even a mini skirt, and still be viewed as decent,
even wholesome.
For me, mini skirts are daring—hiding
while revealing and provoking the imagination.
I'll never wear one.

What a woman wears is but a stitch
in freedom's full attire.

It's true, sometimes, a dress can transform a person,
almost like magic. Years ago, the blue dress
Lenore sewed for me helped me get the job
in Sheridan that changed my life.
How is it anything we wear
holds that kind of magic?

Today's world has moved beyond me,
or I beyond it.
The body changes.
What a woman wants changes with time,
is more complex than the amount of fabric
subtracted or added to her skirt.

I look in the mirror now and wish for the freedom
to greet my body's sagging skin, chipped tooth
and thinning hair and say there's nothing missing,
want to affirm that in my weakness and declining
strength I'm still whole the way the earth is whole
even as it erodes—ice and wind etching the land,
year by year its body slowly carried elsewhere.
That's a different kind of freedom.

My 90-year-old neighbor comes to my door
to tell me his newspaper went missing this morning.
During the conversation, I recognize a humming
beneath the surface of his voice. An old longing rises—
my endless wish to slip inside someone's arms
as if into a river, an immersive presence washing over
and through histories and scars. No judgments.
Just the texture of breath and skin.

The clock ticks by the loud news of its lonely minutes.
I get out a bowl and fold together the ingredients
for noodles, roll the dough smooth, remembering
Mama's words to not measure too much.

Late afternoon I sit in my chair with my cat, Sable,
gazing out the window, imagining
the Laramie Mountains' snowy heights
waiting in the distance, just past what I can see.

Bird, bear, or wild iris—there are many bodies
I might someday become after my body
returns to earth. My story is longer
than the life I've lived,
larger than my longings.

I wrap around me the blue shawl
my great-niece in California made,
prepare for another transformation.

STANDING IN THE MIDDLE
OF A GREAT FIELD

Cheyenne, Wyoming, 1983
Adah, age 94

A sea of wheat—tall, thin stalks swaying, bending.
Unable, like me, to escape the earth it stands in,

wheat leans into incessant wind. I went there often
to hide when young, climbed inside its cover,

wheat grass forest-thick, reaching to touch
my shoulders. I could see no one.

Neither could they see me.
I could cry, shout, scream and no one

would know. The grass absorbed it all.
An endless soughing of strands, the subtle

rearrangement of wheat reeds.
A million tendrils lift in a gust of air to flutter

momentarily. Then their heads drop—their movement
a kind of breathing, a communal relief, and release.

Held there, sky unfolding forever, universe laid bare,
enveloped in its breadth, nothing hidden, I was

but one thin leaf in the prairie's huge embrace,
bending and blending into its expansive grace.

Disappointment and despair, everything secret
I believed I could never tell anyone, were single threads

in the prairie's great cloak of grass and sky.
The prairie helped me endure

my father's exacting rules, to survive a pregnancy
I didn't choose, the worlds I lost

with my husbands' deaths, and it helps me now
I am alone, expecting what's coming next.

My roots are in a field of wind and sun,
feet planted firm in deep earth.

TIMELINE

1847	Jasper is born in Iowa
1850	World population reaches 1,271,000,000
1857	Adella is born in Indiana
1858–1861	Gold is discovered in southwestern Nebraska Territory
1860–1861	Pony Express crosses the Great Plains to Sacramento, California
1861–1865	American Civil War
1861–1900	Five US transcontinental railroads come into existence
1863	First Nebraska claim under the Homestead Act is staked near Beatrice
1865	Building of the first railroad to the Pacific Coast begins in Omaha
1867	Nebraska becomes a state
1867	Fort Russell, later known as Warren Air Force Base, is built west of Cheyenne, Wyoming
1869	As a US territory, the Wyoming Territorial Assembly grants women the right to vote
1869	Railroad to the Pacific Coast is completed
1875	Gold is discovered in South Dakota's Black Hills
1870	Louisa Swain of Laramie, Wyoming, is the first woman in the US to vote
1871	Amalia Post successfully persuades Wyoming's governor Campbell to not repeal women's right to vote in Wyoming
1877	On May 6, Chief Crazy Horse and 900 warriors surrender at Camp Robinson, Nebraska
1877	Jasper and Adella marry and homestead east of Crawford, Nebraska
1879	Rhoda is born
1881	Shara is born
1882	Cheyenne, Wyoming, is named the wealthiest city per capita in the world

1883	Swan Land and Cattle Company is organized, trading land, sheep, cattle, and horses in western US
1883	Lenore is born
1885	Rhoda dies of whooping cough
1885	Dawes County, Nebraska, is organized, containing 1,404 square miles, much of which is clay loam and untillable
1886	The Fremont, Elkhorn, and Missouri Valley Railroad comes to Fort Robinson in northwestern Nebraska, giving birth to Crawford
1886	Leith is born
1886–1887	A harsh winter, known as the Big Die-Up, brings an end to the open range era
1887	The Dawes Act is passed, causing Native Americans to lose 65% of their land and the elimination of Tribal governments
1889	Chicago, Burlington and Quincy Railroad builds lines through Crawford, Nebraska, causing industries to expand to include brick works, a mica mill, and a pickle factory
1889	Adah is born
1890	Jasper and family start homesteading east of Crawford, Nebraska
1890	US Government suppresses the Lakota Sioux Ghost Dance on South Dakota reservations, leading to the Wounded Knee Massacre
1890	Wyoming is admitted to the US and is the first state in the Union to allow women to vote
1892	Burlington and Missouri River Railroad arrives in Sheridan, Wyoming
1893	Sheridan Inn completed in Sheridan, Wyoming
1893	Avery is born in Crawford, Nebraska
1895	Edra is born in Crawford, Nebraska
1897	Jamie is born in Crawford, Nebraska
1897	Adah goes to work at the Hughes's home
1898	Spanish American War

1899	Cedric is born in Crawford, Nebraska
1899	Lenore works as a dishwasher in Crawford, Nebraska
1900	Shara dies
1900	Married women gain some control over their property and earnings in every US state
1902	Clothes brought by train and horse and wagon to those on the Great Plains
1903	Wright brothers' first flight
1905	Lenore is living in Newcastle, Wyoming
1905	Adah marries Claude and soon after annuls the marriage
1906	Lenore marries Jed, (born in Pennsylvania) in Weston, Wyoming; she is 25, he is 45
1907	Adah moves to Weston, Wyoming to live with Lenore and Jed
1908	Wyoming leads US in wool production with over six million sheep valued at $32 million
1908	Margot is born in Weston, Wyoming
1908	Lenore and Jed adopt Margot
1909	Adah moves to Sheridan, Wyoming
1909	Armed men kill three men in a sheep camp—roast two in the sheep wagon and shoot the third—and kill the dogs near Spring Creek, south of Ten Sleep, Wyoming
1909	Adah marries Gerard in Sheridan, Wyoming
1910	Value of Wyoming cattle reaches $262 million
1910	Last year of the Swan Land and Cattle Company's joint cattle and sheep operation
1910	Electric streetcar line opens in Sheridan, Wyoming
1910	Adah's family is renting in Bordeaux, Laramie County, Wyoming
1911	Swan Land and Cattle Company has 112,000 head of sheep
1911	Harsh winter in Wyoming decimates sheep flocks

1911	Adah and Gerard move to Des Moines, Iowa; Gerard learns carpentry
1913	Ford initiates the first assembly line for mass production of the automobile
1914	World War I starts in Europe
1915	Adah and Gerard move to Cheyenne, Wyoming
1915	Leith marries Brielle
1916	Edra marries August in Wheatland, Wyoming; they met at Two Bar Ranch, Wheatland, part of the Swan Company
1916	Adah and Gerard are living in Cheyenne
1917–1918	US enters World War I
1918	World War I ends
1918	Jasper dies at age 71 in Chugwater, Wyoming
1918	Worldwide pandemic
1919	19th constitutional amendment ratified; women attain right to vote
1919	Chugwater, Wyoming, incorporated
1919	Gerard buys property in Cheyenne; Adah works at Fort Russell laundry
1920	Cheyenne Regional Airport opens, serving as a stop for airmail
1920s	Specialization of specific single crops on farms increases, along with modernization and mechanization
1921–1929	101 of Wyoming's 153 banks fail
1922	Adella marries Joel (Swiss heritage)
1924	Leith and Brielle adopt Kent
1924	Native Americans granted citizenship, given legal rights for the first time
1924	Hubble reveals the existence of other galaxies
1924	All-purpose tractor introduced by International Harvester
1925	American Indian suffrage granted
1925	Jamie marries Howard

1926	Swan Land and Cattle Company separates from British charter and establishes the Swan Company, headquartered in Chugwater, Wyoming, focusing on sheep breeding, wool production, and grazing lands
1926	Jamie divorces Howard
1926	Jamie marries Frank
1927	Cedric marries Della
1928	Jamie divorces Frank
1928	Jamie marries Alfred
1929	US stock market crashes
1930	At least one tractor is owned on each of the 3,749 farms in Wyoming
1930–1936	Drought in Wyoming
1930–1940	Great Depression, worldwide depression, Dust Bowl
1931	Frank (Jamie's second husband) dies
1931	Outbreak of flightless grasshopper, associated with severe drought
1932	The National Recovery Act allows only one family member to hold a government job.
1933	Civilian Conservation Corps is created, paying men to work in forests and grazing communities to plant trees and build trails and livestock facilities
1933	Record low temperatures of -66 F in Yellowstone National Park
1934	Taylor Grazing Act requires permits and fees for grazing animals on public land
1935	Adella dies in Chugwater, Wyoming
1935	Gerard dies in Cheyenne, Wyoming; married 27 years to Adah
1935	Cedric and Della adopt a daughter
1936	Adah marries Raymond
1936	Adah divorces Raymond
1937	Adah marries Litton

1937	Population outbreak of crickets causes $375,000 of crop damage in Wyoming
1938	Peak year of cricket invasion affects 19 million acres of crops; 11 states devoured
1938	The Fair Labor Standards Act establishes a minimum wage, helping to reduce gender pay disparities
1939	World War II begins when Germany invades Poland
1939	First TV broadcast
1942	Cedric and Della adopt a second daughter
1942	Branches created in the armed forces allowing women to join the war effort
1942	People of Japanese, Italian, and German ancestry living in the US are forced into internment camps
1945	Atomic bombs dropped on Japan, World War II ends
1945–1960	Use of chemical fertilizers, pesticides, herbicides, and antibiotics in agriculture increases
1945–1960	Number of farms in Wyoming seriously declines
1948	Lenore dies in Newcastle, Wyoming
1949	Most serious blizzard since 1886 hits Wyoming, Nebraska, South Dakota, and Colorado, incurring 190 million dollars' worth of damage
1950–1953	5.7 million Americans served in the Korean War with 1.8 million military personnel in active combat
1954	Pivot irrigation systems are developed
1950–1960	Interstate highways are built
1955	Adah and Litton move to Mesa, Arizona
1957	Elizabeth Eckford attends school at the previously all-white Central High School in Little Rock, Arkansas, along with eight other Black students known as the Little Rock Nine
1960	First oral contraceptive is approved by the FDA
1963	The Equal Pay Act is signed into law; promises wages equal wages regardless of religion, color, race, national origin, or gender of worker
1964	Civil Rights Act signed into law

1965	Mary Quant designs the mini-skirt in London
1965	Litton dies in Mesa, Arizona; Adah moves back to Cheyenne, Wyoming
1966	Race riots in Omaha, Nebraska
1967	Leith dies
1968	Martin Luther King Jr., Civil Rights leader, is assassinated
1969	US astronauts land on the moon
1971	Edra dies
1972	Cedric's wife Della dies
1972	Avery dies
1972	Cedric marries Della's sister Ava
1973	The Committee to End Sterilization Abuse is created
1973	US Supreme Court decision on Roe v Wade declares abortion a constitutional right
1974	Barbara Walters becomes first female evening news anchor
1978	First test tube baby born
1979	Department of Health, Education, and Welfare requires informed consent for sterilization procedures
1981	Cedric dies
1981	First woman selected for the Supreme Court—Judge Sandra Day O'Connor
1983	Sally Ride is the first American woman in space
1986	Adah dies in Cheyenne at age 96
1987	Jamie dies
1987	World population reaches 5 billion

AFTERWORD

A Few Snapshots

I. Crawford, Nebraska

A wild town with dirt streets busy with saloons and brothels, the Fort Robinson's soldiers came into Crawford looking for excitement. Calamity Jane put up a tent south of town and brought in dancing girls from Deadwood, South Dakota, adding to the town's raucous character. Crawford was a German POW camp in World War II.

II. Sheridan, Wyoming

When the Burlington & Missouri River Railroad arrived in Sheridan in 1892, it boosted the town's economy. In the 1910s, Sheridan had electric lights, water works, soda drink manufacturers, cigar factories, hotels with steam heat, and the only long-distance electric trolley line in the state. Nearby mines at Dietz, Monarch, and Acme, along Goose Creek and in the Tongue River Valley, brought in people from Poland, Italy, Greece, Germany, Mexico, Japan, and Pakistan, lending Sheridan an international atmosphere.

III. Cheyenne, Wyoming

Cheyenne was a supply center for war with the Sioux and later for Black Hills miners. Money poured into cattle barons' deep pockets. In 1882 Cheyenne was the wealthiest city per capita in the world. Electric lights brightened streets, and the city had an opera house and a men's club with fine food, liquor, and fancy cigars. Things seemed good until 1886 and 1887 when subzero temperatures and blizzards killed thousands of cattle in what is referred to as the Great Die-Up.

IV. Fort Russell

Fort Russell was built west of Cheyenne, Wyoming, in 1867 to protect railroad construction crews from Native people settlers viewed as hostile. Businesses, real estate investors, and gamblers followed, with hopes for wealth and profit. Violence was a way of life. Six months after Cheyenne became a city, Rev. Cook said, "The wickedness is unimaginable and appalling." Havoc and hell in motion defined the town. Laws were mostly a suggestion, vigilantes the mode. "Pistols are almost as numerous as men," reported one newspaper editor. A central training center during World War I, Fort Russell was renamed Warren Air Force Base and expanded. It is America's oldest continuously active Air Force base and is considered the most modern missile facility in the US.

V.   Swan Cattle Company

For nearly seventy years, the Swan Land and Cattle Company, founded in 1883, influenced lives across Wyoming. The company held 4.5 million acres in Wyoming and had over 100,000 head of cattle. At its peak, the company was worth the equivalent of 60 to 67 million dollars in today's money. Overgrazing and overcrowding animals at that time was less important than people's desire for making money. After the severe winter of 1886–87, known as the Great Die-Up, the era of raising cattle on the open range ended. The company lost over half of their cattle and falsified their books as well. Their power diminished, and the company separated from their British owners, reorganized, brought in new management, and focused on raising sheep instead.

VI. Wyoming Winter

In 1949 Wyoming experienced one of the worst winters on record. Arctic wind, pounding snow, drifts up to thirty feet high, and sub-zero temperatures stranded people and animals for days while many were also trapped in their homes and barns. Supplies running short, people wrote messages in the snow requesting help. Planes and convoys brought hay to ranch animals. Meanwhile, roofs collapsed and snow fell through cracks in boards, filling homes and barns with snow. Animals died standing upright, frozen in their tracks.

 ANNA CITRINO grew up in San Diego County, California. She received her MA from the Bread Loaf School of English in Vermont and taught abroad in Turkey, Kuwait, Singapore, Saudi Arabia, India, and the United Kingdom. Her work has appeared in *Bellowing Ark*, *Canary*, *Indelible*, *Juniper*, *Lips*, *Main Street Rag*, *Paterson Literary Review*, *Poppy Road Review*, *Spillway*, and *Still Point Arts Quarterly*, among numerous other journals and anthologies. Citrino is the author of two chapbooks, *Saudade*, and *To Find a River*, as well as two books, *A Space Between*, and *Buoyant*. One of her poems was nominated for a Pushcart Prize in 2019. Citrino is an avid walker, scuba diver, and bicyclist. Currently, she lives in Sonoma County, California, where she's learning to draw trees and is working with her husband, Michael, to make their backyard garden a wonderland of beauty and food to share with others. Find her on Instagram at ajcitrino and read more of her writing at annacitrino.com.

Shanti Arts

Nature · Art · Spirit

Please visit us online
to browse our entire book catalog,
including poetry collections and fiction,
books on travel, nature, healing, art,
photography, and more.

Also take a look at our highly regarded art
and literary journal, *Still Point Arts Quarterly*,
which may be downloaded for free.

www.shantiarts.com

www.ingramcontent.com/pod-product-compliance
Lightning Source LLC
Chambersburg PA
CBHW020227170426
43201CB00007B/346